How to Make Money Online Fast

This work from home hustle could net you over $3000 per month in just 3 hours a day!

Mel Eids

Copyright © 2024 by Mel Eids

All rights reserved. No portion of this book may be reproduced in any form without written permission from the publisher or author, except as permitted by U.S. copyright law.

Legal Notice:

This publication is designed to provide accurate and authoritative information in regard to the subject matter covered. It is sold with the understanding that neither the author nor the publisher is engaged in rendering legal, investment, accounting or other professional services. While the publisher and author have used their best efforts in preparing this book, they make no representations or warranties with respect to the accuracy or completeness of the contents of this book and specifically disclaim any implied warranties of merchantability or fitness for a particular purpose. No warranty may be created or extended by sales representatives or written sales materials. The advice and strategies contained herein may not be suitable for your situation. You should consult with a professional when appropriate.

Disclaimer Notice:

The information provided in this book is for entertainment purposes only. While every effort has been made to ensure the accuracy and completeness of the information contained in this text, the author and publisher make no guarantee and assume no responsibility for any errors, omissions, or inaccuracies found herein. Neither the author nor the publisher shall be liable for any direct, indirect, incidental, consequential, or punitive damages arising out of your access to, use of, or reliance on the information contained in this book. The reader is responsible for their own actions and decisions, and the use of this book's content is at the reader's own risk.

ISBN: 9781963075120

First Edition

Introduction 7

Chapter 1: Understanding Online Marketplaces 17

Chapter 2: Where to Get the Stuff to Sell? 31

Chapter 3: Selling on eBay 63

Chapter 4: Selling on Amazon 75

Chapter 5: Selling on OfferUp 89

Chapter 6: Selling on Facebook Marketplace 107

Chapter 7: Selling on Etsy 127

Chapter 8: Cross-Platform Selling Strategies 141

Resources 157

    Cross Platform Selling Resources 158

    Pricing Resources 159

    SEO Resources 159

    Educational Resources 160

    Tools and Apps for Online Selling 160

    Resources for Sourcing Products 161

Introduction

Hi! My name is **Mel**, and I'd like to share my story with you. Through my journey, I've learned valuable lessons about making money online, particularly by selling tangible goods on various platforms. In this book, I'll be focusing on the platforms I've become an expert in: eBay, Amazon, OfferUp, Facebook Marketplace, and Etsy.

But before we get to the nitty-gritty of online selling, let me tell you a bit about my background. In my mid-30s, I found myself working for various home improvement companies, helping them with their marketing efforts. It was an exciting time, especially when I joined a tiny startup that, over the course of four years, grew so big that it caught the eye of an investment firm. However, with growth came change, and the company had to trim its budget. As one of the highest-paid employees, I found myself laid off, having trained my own replacements. That just sucked. They were bought by one of the "Big Boys" in our space and I didn't get to go on the ride. More importantly, I couldn't put the new name on the resume. I had to start over.

The layoff was **devastating**. I felt like I had lost something I had helped build from the ground up. But, rather than wallow, I decided to take control of my future. With no formal education to fall back on, I made the bold decision to go back to school. I enrolled in an associate's degree program, which eventually led to a bachelor's and then a master's degree. I hustled on this with the help of an online program. I got lucky. The online school was under a prestigious name. It looks great on the resume. It took me 3.5 years to finish the Master's in Business Administration with a concentration in Marketing.

Pursuing higher education was a good experience, but it also came with its own set of challenges. I had to find ways to pay for school while also covering all of my bills and taking care of my toddler. It was a daunting task, but it was also the catalyst that led me to discover various ways to make money online. The best part? Most of these methods didn't even require me to leave the house, and I was my own boss. After all, you can't fire yourself!

Spoiler alert: After I got my Master's degree, I had a hell of a time finding a job. I don't know if it was the employment gap or if they could smell my age. I don't know if they could Google my unique last name and find out that I had a kid. The jobs I was applying for were upper-level management and required a lot of commitment. I can commit, damn it! I'm not going to speculate. I finally found one and stuck with it for over a year. It was low level phone work in a new industry. I hated every second of it. While I was on my long commute, I was educating myself through podcasts on various topics. Though I'm on leave right now to be closer and more available for two ailing parents, I am making more money than I was working full-time for my last company. This, I will teach you.

This brings us to the focus of this book: selling tangible goods online. In today's digital age, the opportunities for making money through online selling are vast and varied. From vintage collectibles to handmade crafts, there's a market for just about everything. And with the rise of e-commerce platforms like eBay, Amazon, Offer Up, Facebook Marketplace, Etsy, and even TikTok Shops, it's easier than ever to reach a wide audience of potential buyers.

But with so many options available, it can be overwhelming to know where to start. That's where this book comes in. As someone who has navigated the world of online selling for years, I've gained valuable insights and expertise that I want to share with you. Whether you're looking to supplement your income, start a side hustle, or even launch a full-time business, this book will provide you with the tools and knowledge you need to succeed.

Disclaimer: I subscribe to a "work smart, not hard" philosophy. Some of you may think of it as taking shortcuts, while others may absolutely love my take on things. However, I can promise all of you one thing: I will not endanger your accounts by telling you to do something that, at the very time of writing this book, is not permitted on each platform. I will provide you with logical, real-world advice to get where you need to go as quickly as possible while doing it responsibly.

We'll dive deep into each of the platforms I mentioned earlier, exploring their unique features, benefits, and challenges. You'll learn how to set up your accounts, create compelling listings, price your items competitively, and market your products effectively.

We'll also cover important topics like shipping and handling, customer service, and dealing with returns and refunds.

This book isn't just about the technical aspects of listing things on these platforms; there are plenty of YouTube videos for that. It's about the mindset and strategies you need to thrive in this space. I'll share my own personal experiences, both the triumphs and the setbacks, and the lessons I've learned along the way. We'll explore the importance of adaptability, persistence, and creativity in the face of challenges, and how to stay motivated and focused on your goals.

We are in this together. With that statement comes your first logical tip: "resale" as a business, has a community, and it is incredibly supportive and wonderful. I suggest you start by connecting on Facebook to resale groups, maybe specifically to your area, so that you can be alerted of BOLOs. For those of you just getting started, BOLO means "be on the lookout." That will help you identify trending products and even where to locate them at great prices to then flip them for an excellent profit. I have made a killing at

Walmart flipping stuff using the "arbitrage" resale model. More to come. :)

One of the biggest advantages of selling tangible goods online is the flexibility it offers. You can work from anywhere, at any time, and on your own terms. Whether you're a stay-at-home parent, a student, or someone looking to escape the 9-to-5 grind, online selling can provide you with the freedom and autonomy you crave. Plus, with the ability to scale your business as you grow, the sky's the limit in terms of earning potential.

But before we get started, I want to emphasize one important point: success in online selling doesn't happen overnight. It takes time, effort, and dedication to build a thriving business. There will be ups and downs, successes and failures, but the key is to stay focused on your goals and keep pushing forward. With the right mindset and the strategies outlined in this book, I'm confident that you can achieve your dreams of financial freedom and independence through online selling.

So, are you ready to embark on this exciting journey? If so, let's dive in and explore the world of selling. Together, we'll uncover the secrets to success on platforms like eBay, Amazon, Offer Up, Facebook Marketplace, and Etsy, and build a thriving business that allows you to live life on your own terms. **You can do this!**

But more than just a how-to guide, this book is a testament to the power of perseverance, adaptability, and creativity in the face of adversity. It's a reminder that no matter where you are in life, there are always opportunities to learn, grow, and succeed. And with the right tools, strategies, and mindset, anyone can achieve their dreams of financial freedom and independence through online selling.

So, if you're ready to take control of your financial future and build a life of freedom and independence, let's get started. The world of online selling awaits, and with the strategies and insights in this book, you'll be well on your way to success.

Please Note: Take the technical aspects of everything I'm saying with a grain of salt. The most important advice I can give you to start your independent money-making journey is to just start. There is a concept called **"analysis paralysis"**. If you suffer from this, you will spend an enormous amount of time trying to make everything perfect. The truth is, which many YouTube gurus won't tell you, is that you can start a company under a sole proprietorship, which means you don't have a formal company structure. Everything that you earn is reported under your personal Social Security number. That is one thing that I don't want you to overlook.

The rest of it is that your listings don't need to be perfect. You don't even know what people out there are really looking for. Just list your items and learn the rules under every platform you're selling on. When it comes to your listings, understand that **your first ones will be your worst ones**. Don't get caught up in making them perfect. Make them as best as you can within a reasonable time frame for your customers. If you look on eBay, for example, you will find a bunch of poorly designed listings... that still sell.

Trust and believe, I suffer from analysis paralysis, and I will sit there, as part of my personality type, and try to make everything perfect. You'll starve to death doing that. **Just get your listings up!**

Chapter 1: Understanding Online Marketplaces

As we start this journey of selling stuff online, it's essential to grasp the different types of online marketplaces available and how to select the right platform for your products and selling style. In this chapter, we'll dig into the various categories of online marketplaces and explore the factors you should consider when choosing the best platform for your business.

Disclaimer: Diversification is key when it comes to selling on different platforms. Not every platform will be suitable for every product type or business strategy. It's essential to read through this book and determine which platforms align best with the products you want to sell. Through my experience trying a little bit of everything, I've discovered that I don't enjoy selling clothes as much as I do selling electronic goods and books. **Relax.** You will figure out your niche. (**niche**: specialized segment of the market for a particular kind of product or service. Choosing a niche involves focusing on a specific area that targets a particular customer base or type of product, rather than attempting to cater to a broader market. This specialization can make it easier to become an expert in the area, establish a loyal customer base, and stand out from competitors.)

Spoiler Alert: As of today, I sell on 7 different platforms. :)

As you explore different product categories, you may find that listing certain items is enjoyable, while listing others feels tedious, and you might find yourself procrastinating as long as possible. This procrastination can lead to what we in the resale industry call a **"death pile"** – an accumulation of unlisted inventory. I strongly urge you to keep your death pile in check from the very beginning of your reselling journey. Trust me, you'll thank yourself later.

Here are some basic product categories to consider:

1. **Electronics**
   - Mobile phones and accessories
   - Computers and tablets
   - Cameras and photography gear
   - Audio equipment and headphones
   - Video games and consoles

2. **Home Goods**
   - Furniture
   - Decorative items
   - Kitchen appliances
   - Bedding and bath items
   - Tools and home improvement

3. **Clothing and Accessories**
   - Women's, men's, and children's clothing

- Shoes
- Bags and purses
- Jewelry and watches
- Sunglasses and hats

4. **Sports and Outdoor Equipment**

    - Bicycles and accessories
    - Fitness equipment
    - Camping gear
    - Sporting goods (like balls, bats, and rackets)
    - Winter sports equipment

5. **Toys and Hobbies**

    - Board games and puzzles
    - Collectibles (e.g., figurines, cards)
    - Model kits and craft supplies
    - Drones and remote-controlled vehicles

- Educational toys

6. **Books and Media**

    - Books (novels, textbooks, cookbooks)

    - DVDs and Blu-ray discs

    - Vinyl records and CDs

    - Magazines and comic books

    - Video games and software

7. **Beauty and Health Products**

    - Skincare products

    - Makeup

    - Haircare products

    - Fragrances

    - Health supplements

8. **Baby and Child Care Products**

    - Baby clothing and shoes

- Nursery furniture
- Strollers and car seats
- Baby toys
- Feeding supplies

9. **Pet Supplies**

    - Pet food and treats
    - Beds and furniture
    - Toys and play equipment
    - Grooming products
    - Aquariums and accessories

10. **Art and Collectibles**

    - Paintings and prints
    - Sculptures
    - Handmade crafts
    - Antiques

Each category offers unique opportunities for resale, depending on market demand, availability, and your own expertise in identifying valuable items. As you navigate the world of online reselling, remember to stay open to trying new categories and platforms, while also being mindful of your personal preferences and strengths.

Types of Online Marketplaces:

1. Auction Sites:

Auction sites, such as eBay, provide sellers with the opportunity to list items for a specific duration, allowing buyers to place bids and compete for the product. The highest bidder at the end of the auction emerges victorious and secures the item. It's important to note that eBay also offers fixed-price listings, giving sellers the flexibility to set a predetermined price for their items. **Additionally**, eBay's "Best Offer" feature enables sellers to accept offers from potential buyers, fostering a dynamic and negotiable selling environment.

Please note: In addition to the auction format, eBay offers a "Buy It Now" feature, which allows you to list your item at a fixed price. This means that buyers can purchase your item immediately at the listed price without going through the bidding process. You also have the option to enable the "Best Offer" feature alongside the "Buy It Now" price, which lets buyers submit offers for you to consider. This flexibility in listing formats makes eBay a versatile platform, catering to different selling preferences and strategies.

Auction sites are particularly well-suited for unique, rare, or high-demand items that have the potential to sell for prices exceeding their listed value. They also cater to sellers who thrive on the excitement and unpredictability of auction-style selling. The competitive nature of auctions can drive up prices, potentially leading to higher profits for sellers.

When using a site like eBay, you can set a reserve price for your auction listings. A reserve price is the minimum amount you're willing to sell your item for. If the reserve price isn't met by the end of the auction, you're not obligated to sell the item. This feature provides protection against selling your item for less than its value, giving you more control over the auction process. However, keep in mind that eBay charges an additional fee for using the reserve price feature, which is non-refundable even if your item doesn't sell. Alternatively, you can set a higher starting price for your auction to discourage low-ball bids without incurring the extra fee.

However, it's crucial to consider the level of effort and time required to monitor and manage auction listings. Sellers must be prepared to answer questions from potential buyers, keep track of bids, and ensure timely shipping once the auction concludes. Additionally, the success of an auction largely depends on the item's desirability and the effectiveness of the listing's presentation.

I've been selling on eBay since 1999, and one thing I've learned is that people who ask a ton of questions and want you to dig into the nitty-gritty of an item, including specific, off-the-wall measurements, are usually not the ones who end up buying. As a reseller, you need to discern between interested parties and nitpickers. Nitpickers rarely make a purchase, while interested parties do. After a bit of experience, you'll be able to distinguish between the two.

If you do a good job creating your listing, including detailed photographs, potential buyers shouldn't have many questions. If they do have questions, they should be unique, one-off inquiries that make you think, "Oh, maybe I missed that in the listing." However, if they ask questions like, "What is the length of the arm from the inner wrist to the elbow crease?" then they might not be the one who ends up buying the item.

Imagine if you have a popular item and you receive five similar questions a day. You'd have to pull that item out of storage, bust out your tape measure, measure it, and respond to each question. Learn how to differentiate between serious buyers and casual browsers. This skill will come with experience. Trust me. :)

2. Direct Sales Platforms:

Direct sales platforms, such as Amazon and Etsy, provide sellers with a straightforward approach to listing items at a fixed price. Buyers can purchase products instantly without the need for bidding, making the transaction process more streamlined and efficient. These platforms are ideal for sellers who prefer a more predictable and consistent pricing structure, as well as those who value simplicity in their selling process.

One of the primary advantages of direct sales platforms is their extensive user base. Platforms like Amazon boast millions of active customers, providing sellers with unparalleled visibility and potential reach for their products. This increased exposure can lead to higher sales volume and a steady stream of income.

However, it's important to note that direct sales platforms often have more stringent requirements and guidelines for sellers. Amazon, for example, has specific criteria for product listings, including detailed descriptions, high-quality images, and accurate categorization. Sellers must adhere to these standards to maintain their seller accounts in good standing.

Etsy, on the other hand, caters specifically to handmade, vintage, and unique items. Sellers on Etsy must ensure that their products align with the platform's focus on creativity and authenticity. This niche market can be advantageous for sellers who specialize in one-of-a-kind or artisanal products, as it attracts a specific customer base seeking those types of items.

Please note: Although Etsy initially positioned itself as a platform focused on handmade items, it has significantly deviated from that business model over the years. Currently, Etsy allows sellers who engage in drop shipping and those who sell imported, non-handmade goods. While this may not align with Etsy's original vision and public perception, it is the reality on the platform today.

To succeed on Etsy with non-handmade items, it's crucial to differentiate your product and avoid engaging in a race to the bottom on price. By offering unique, high-quality items and providing excellent customer service, you can still be successful on the platform, even if your products are not entirely handmade.

Additionally, Etsy freely accepts crafting supplies on the platform as well as Vintage items. If you're interested in selling supplies that could be used for crafting, such as beads, fabric, or tools, Etsy may be the ideal marketplace for you. The platform's audience includes many crafters and DIY enthusiasts who are actively seeking supplies for their projects.

3. Community Marketplaces:

Community marketplaces, such as Facebook Marketplace and OfferUp, prioritize local connections, enabling sellers to interact directly with buyers in their vicinity. These platforms are particularly well-suited for items that are impractical or costly to ship, such as furniture, appliances, or bulky home goods. By facilitating in-person transactions, community marketplaces eliminate the need for shipping arrangements and associated expenses.

One of the key benefits of community marketplaces is the sense of trust and familiarity they foster between buyers and sellers. When transactions occur face-to-face, both parties have the opportunity to assess the item's condition, discuss any concerns, and build a rapport. This personal interaction can lead to a smoother and more satisfying selling experience.

However, it's crucial to prioritize safety when engaging in in-person transactions. Always meet in a well-lit, public location, and consider bringing along a friend or family member for added security. Be cautious when sharing personal information and trust your instincts if a situation feels uncomfortable or suspicious.

Personally, I have met buyers at local parks and even my local police station. It's better to be safe than sorry.

While there is an element of risk involved in selling on community marketplaces for local pickup, there are also some advantages, such as the fact that these transactions are often conducted in cash. This can be convenient and helps avoid potential issues with payment processing or chargebacks. However, it's important to note that even though these are cash transactions, you are still obligated to report this income on your taxes. Failing to do so could lead to legal consequences down the road.

Remember, your safety and well-being should always be your top priority when engaging in local transactions. By taking the necessary precautions and being aware of potential risks, you can enjoy the benefits of selling on community marketplaces while minimizing your exposure to dangerous situations.

Chapter 2: Where to Get the Stuff to Sell?

Do prepare yourself; **this chapter will be beefy.** You can always come back to this later after you have learned about the various platforms. Ultimately, you will most likely discover through trial and error what you enjoy selling. Very few resellers enjoy everything. As a matter of fact, I don't know a single reseller who enjoys selling in every category. They usually have their darlings and acquiesce to selling in a few other categories based on the availability of the items. Personally, I love hard goods and small electronics. I hate selling clothes. I know some folks who make a killing in clothes; listing clothes is way too tedious for me and my personality type. So, look at this chapter as a way to spark ideas for gathering inventory. **Reference it later**, even come back to it if you think you have tapped out all of the avenues that you can initially think of. I guarantee you there is some gold here for you.

In the world of ecommerce, finding the right products to sell is crucial to the success of your online business. With so many options available, it can be overwhelming to know where to start. In this chapter, we will explore over 30 different places where you can source items to sell online, beginning with the most accessible option: your own home.

1. Your Home

One of the easiest places to start sourcing products for your ecommerce business is right under your own roof. Take a look around your home and identify items that you no longer use or need. These could include:

a. Clothing and accessories

b. Books, movies, and music

c. Electronics and gadgets

d. Furniture and home décor

e. Sports equipment and outdoor gear

f. Collectibles and vintage items

By selling items you already own, you can kick-start your e-commerce business with minimal upfront investment. If you're starting this venture with no money, this is a great place to start. This will allow you to source more inventory with the proceeds and grow.

2. Friends and Family

Reach out to your friends and family members to see if they have any items they'd like to sell. Many people have unwanted gifts, impulse purchases, or items they no longer use that they'd be happy to part with. You can offer to sell these items on their behalf and split the profits, creating a win-win situation for both parties.

> **I've approached this in two different ways.** The first method involves offering my services for a commission, which can yield good results depending on the item and category. Initially, I focused on eBay and OfferUp. Just make sure you are being upfront about them needing to cover the fees, then pay the commission. Keep it clear and honest. Let them know what the fees are and what your commission rate is. You can even give them a link to the eBay auction so that

they can watch it. Make sure they understand how the listing will work if you are putting it as an auction with or without a reserve or if it will be a buy-it-now listing. If you are willing to take offers, make sure you know what they are willing to let it go for. The second approach was to inform my family about my venture and inquire if they had any unused items they were willing to donate to kickstart my reselling business. Consequently, my parents closed a storage unit and contributed hundreds of dollars' worth of inventory to me.

3. Garage Sales and Yard Sales

Attending garage sales and yard sales in your local area can be a great way to find unique and affordable items to resell online. Keep an eye out for underpriced or high-demand items that you can purchase and list on your e-commerce platform for a profit. You will often find me at garage sales with **my phone in my hand**, looking up items on eBay to see what they have sold for. That's a little tip for you: when you look up an item there, **filter by sold and completed.** After all, something is only worth what someone is willing to pay for it, and if you just look at the items that are listed, it doesn't give you the whole picture. Perhaps the market is flooded with something that nobody wants. Also, be mindful of the sell-through rate. The search results that you are seeing are for a rolling 90 days.

4. Thrift Stores and Consignment Shops

Thrift stores and consignment shops are treasure troves for sourcing products. These establishments often carry a wide variety of items at discounted prices, including clothing, furniture, books, and household goods. Regularly visit these stores to find hidden gems that you can resell online.

Note about Goodwill:

Before anything hits the store shelves, Goodwill employees go through all the donations and **cherry-pick** the best stuff to sell on their own website and eBay store. Many other thrift stores do this, including ones that are nonprofit. The trick is to check out the ones in your area and look for the diamonds in the rough. In order to find the goods, you have to go out and survey the landscape. There's no one-size-fits-all solution for this. You have to check your stores.

5. Flea Markets and Swap Meets

Flea markets and swap meets are popular venues for finding unique and vintage items. Vendors at these events often sell a wide range of products, from antiques and collectibles to handmade crafts and artisanal goods. Strike up conversations with sellers to learn more about their products and negotiate better prices for bulk purchases.

6. Estate Sales and Auctions

Estate sales and auctions are excellent sources for sourcing high-quality, unique items. These events often occur when someone is downsizing, moving, or after a person has passed away. You can find valuable items such as antique furniture, rare books, jewelry, and artwork at these sales, which you can then resell online for a profit.

Online auction sites, including those that specialize in **storage unit** auctions, can be a fantastic resource for sourcing inventory for your ecommerce business. These platforms offer a wide variety of items, often at competitive prices, and can be a treasure trove for unique, high-demand products. Storage unit auctions, in particular, can yield an eclectic mix of goods, from furniture and appliances to collectibles and vintage items.

However, it's crucial to be aware that **cherry-picking** may occur in these online auction environments. Just like with Goodwill, some sellers may carefully sort through the contents of a storage unit before listing it for auction, removing the most valuable items to sell separately. This practice can leave bidders with a less desirable selection of products, potentially impacting the profitability of your sourcing efforts.

To navigate this challenge, consider the following tips:

1. Research the seller's history and feedback ratings to gauge their reputation and the quality of the auctions they host.

2. Carefully review the auction photos and descriptions to assess the condition and potential value of the items being sold.

3. Set a budget and stick to it, avoiding the temptation to engage in bidding wars that may drive prices beyond your profit margins.

4. Factor in additional costs such as shipping, storage, and any necessary repairs or cleaning when determining your maximum bid.

5. Diversify your sourcing strategy by exploring multiple online auction sites and sellers to increase your chances of finding profitable inventory.

By keeping these **considerations in mind** and approaching online auctions with a strategic mindset, you can successfully leverage these platforms to source products for your ecommerce business while minimizing the impact of cherry-picking.

7. Liquidation Sales and Closeouts

Liquidation sales and closeouts happen when businesses are looking to quickly sell off their inventory, often due to store closures, overstocking, or product discontinuation. These sales can be a great opportunity to purchase products at a fraction of their retail price, which you can then resell on your ecommerce platform.

There are several ways to **find out about liquidation sales** and closeouts for sourcing products:

1. Online liquidation marketplaces: Websites like Liquidation.com, DirectLiquidation.com, and BulkLoads.com specialize in connecting buyers with businesses looking to sell their excess inventory, customer returns, or overstock items.

2. Liquidation auctions: Online auction sites such as AuctionNation.com, Bid4Assets.com, and GovDeals.com often feature liquidation sales from businesses, government agencies, and other organizations.

3. Retailer websites: Many large retailers, such as Walmart, Amazon, and Target, have dedicated liquidation sections on their websites where they sell returned, refurbished, or overstock items at discounted prices.

4. Wholesale suppliers: Some wholesale suppliers and distributors offer liquidation sales and closeout deals to their customers. Research and connect with wholesalers in your niche to stay informed about these opportunities.

5. Social media: Follow retailers, brands, and liquidation companies on social media platforms like Facebook, Twitter, and Instagram to stay updated on any upcoming sales or special deals.

6. Email newsletters: Sign up for email newsletters from liquidation marketplaces, retailers, and suppliers to receive notifications about closeout sales and special promotions directly in your inbox.

7. Industry publications and blogs: Read trade publications, magazines, and blogs related to your niche or the retail industry to stay informed about liquidation sales and closeout opportunities.

8. Business relationships: Build relationships with store managers, suppliers, and other business owners in your network, as they may be able to provide insider information on upcoming liquidation events or excess inventory sales.

By proactively seeking out information from these various sources, you can stay informed about liquidation sales and closeouts that may offer valuable inventory for your ecommerce business.

8. Wholesale Suppliers and Distributors

Partnering with wholesale suppliers and distributors is a popular way to source products for your ecommerce business. These companies specialize in selling products in bulk at discounted prices, allowing you to purchase inventory at a lower cost and resell it for a profit. Research and reach out to wholesalers and distributors in your niche to establish a business relationship.

There are several ways to find and connect with wholesale suppliers and distributors for your ecommerce business:

1. Online directories: Websites like Worldwide Brands, SaleHoo, and Wholesale Central maintain extensive directories of verified wholesale suppliers and distributors across various industries and niches.

2. Trade shows and exhibitions: Attending trade shows and exhibitions specific to your niche is an excellent way to meet wholesale suppliers and distributors in person, see products firsthand, and establish business relationships.

3. Industry associations and networks: Join industry-specific associations, networks, or groups to access member directories, attend events, and connect with potential suppliers and distributors in your niche.

4. Manufacturer websites: Visit the websites of manufacturers whose products you're interested in selling. Many manufacturers have wholesale or distributor programs and can provide information on how to become an authorized reseller.

5. Online marketplaces: Platforms like Alibaba, Global Sources, and DHgate connect buyers with wholesale suppliers and distributors, primarily from Asia. However, be sure to thoroughly vet suppliers and request product samples before placing large orders.

6. Referrals and recommendations: Reach out to other business owners, ecommerce entrepreneurs, or industry contacts for referrals and recommendations on reliable wholesale suppliers and distributors they've worked with.

7. Search engines: Use search engines like Google to find potential suppliers and distributors. Search for terms like "[your niche] wholesale supplier," "[product] distributor," or "[brand name] wholesale" to find relevant results.

8. LinkedIn: Utilize LinkedIn to search for and connect with professionals working for wholesale suppliers and distributors in your industry. Engage with them to learn more

about their products and partnership opportunities.

9. Trade publications and magazines: Read trade publications and magazines related to your niche, as they often feature advertisements and listings for wholesale suppliers and distributors.

10. Dropshipping directories: If you're interested in dropshipping, explore directories like Oberlo, Spocket, and Dropship Direct to find suppliers who offer this fulfillment method.

The point is to reach out. A simple email might do. Say something like: "Hi, I'm looking for XYZ. Do you have a company that you could recommend?"

When contacting potential wholesale suppliers and distributors, be prepared to provide information about your business, such as your company name, website, and resale certificate. Building strong relationships with your suppliers is key to ensuring a reliable supply of products for your e-commerce business.

9. Dropshipping Suppliers

Dropshipping is a fulfillment method where you sell products on your ecommerce platform without actually holding the inventory yourself. When a customer places an order, you purchase the item from a third-party supplier, who then ships the product directly to the customer. This model allows you to offer a wide range of products without the need for upfront inventory investment or storage space.

10. Manufacturers

Connecting with manufacturers directly can be an effective way to source unique or customized products for your ecommerce business. Many manufacturers are willing to work with small businesses and can offer competitive pricing for bulk orders. Attend trade shows or use online directories to find manufacturers in your niche and reach out to them to discuss potential partnerships.

11. Handmade and Crafted Items

If you have a creative skill or hobby, consider making and selling your own handmade or crafted items.

Platforms like Etsy cater specifically to handmade and vintage goods, providing a ready-made audience for your unique creations. You can also sell your handmade items on general ecommerce platforms like Amazon Handmade or your own website.

Note about me: I have had 3D printers for several years now and have recently realized that there is a good amount of money to be made by 3D printing and selling interesting things online. I have recently opened an Etsy shop for this, and I'm also cross-listing on eBay and OfferUp. I love being able to make my own products.

12. Print-on-Demand Services

Print-on-demand services allow you to create and sell customized products without holding any inventory. You simply upload your designs to the platform, and the service handles the printing, packaging, and shipping of the products to your customers. Popular print-on-demand products include t-shirts, mugs, phone cases, and wall art.

Note about me: I am selling T-shirts on Merch by Amazon as well as Etsy that are Print on Demand

(POD). I am designing these graphics on Kittle, Mid Journey, and a little bit of Photoshop.

13. Overstock and Clearance Sections

Many retailers have overstock and clearance sections where they sell products at deeply discounted prices. These items may be end-of-season, returned, or slightly damaged goods that are still in usable condition. Keep an eye out for these deals both in-store and online, as you can often purchase products at a fraction of their original price and resell them for a profit.

14. Online Marketplaces and Classifieds

Online marketplaces and classifieds such as eBay, Facebook Marketplace, and Craigslist can be excellent sources for finding products to resell. People often use these platforms to sell items they no longer need or want, and you can find great deals on a wide variety of products. Be sure to thoroughly inspect the items and communicate clearly with the seller before making a purchase.

This is considered **a type of retail arbitrage**. The purpose of this is to source products for less than you can sell them for and take into account the listing fees that you're paying on the platform where you're flipping. People make a living doing this. There's a lot of tracking and spreadsheets involved to really do it right. The profit margins are slim, and you have to operate in high volume. You can do this in physical stores, which we will describe below. Larger profit margins in many cases.

15. Discount Stores and Dollar Stores

Discount stores and dollar stores offer a wide range of products at extremely low prices, making them an excellent source for retail arbitrage opportunities. **For example**, suppose you come across a popular toy at a dollar store that is selling for $5, but you know that the same toy is being sold on Amazon for $15. By purchasing multiple units of the toy at the dollar store and reselling them on Amazon, you can make a significant profit.

While the quality of items at discount stores may vary, you can often find hidden gems that can be resold for a profit. Keep an eye out for popular or trendy items, as well as products that can be bundled together to create attractive packages for your customers. It's essential to do your research and compare prices across different platforms to ensure that you're making a worthwhile investment.

16. Wholesale Clubs and Membership Stores

Wholesale clubs and membership stores like Costco, Sam's Club, and BJ's Wholesale offer products in bulk at discounted prices. If you have a membership, you can purchase large quantities of popular items and resell them on your ecommerce platform. Be sure to compare prices and factor in shipping costs to ensure that you can still make a profit after reselling the items.

17. Importing from Overseas Suppliers

When considering importing products from overseas suppliers like Alibaba or AliExpress to flip online, there are several important factors to keep in mind to ensure a successful and profitable venture:

1. Product Research: Before placing an order, thoroughly research the product you intend to

sell. Look for items that are in high demand, have low competition, and offer a good profit margin. Use tools like Google Trends, Amazon Best Sellers, and eBay's "Sold Items" feature to gather data on product popularity and pricing.

2. Supplier Verification: Take the time to verify the legitimacy and reliability of the supplier. Check their ratings, reviews, and transaction history on the platform. Communicate with the supplier to assess their responsiveness and professionalism. If possible, request product samples to evaluate the quality firsthand.

3. Pricing and Profitability: When calculating your potential profit, factor in all costs associated with importing and selling the product, such as the item cost, shipping fees, customs duties, platform fees, and marketing expenses. Ensure that your selling price allows for a sufficient profit margin after all these costs are considered.

4. Shipping and Logistics: Understand the shipping options provided by the supplier, including estimated delivery times and tracking capabilities. Be aware that shipping from countries like China can take several weeks, so plan your inventory accordingly. Consider using a fulfillment service like Amazon FBA to streamline your order processing and delivery.

5. Product Compliance: Ensure that the products you import comply with your country's regulations, such as safety standards, labeling requirements, and intellectual property laws. Failure to comply with these regulations can result in your products being seized by customs or your seller account being suspended.

6. Branding and Packaging: To differentiate your products and create a professional image, consider custom branding and packaging. Some suppliers offer these services, or you can arrange for them separately after receiving your inventory.

7. Customer Service: Be prepared to handle customer inquiries, returns, and refunds promptly and professionally. Maintain open communication with your supplier in case you need to address any product issues or reorder inventory.

By carefully researching your products, suppliers, and logistics, importing from overseas suppliers can be a lucrative way to source items for your online flipping business. However, it's crucial to approach this method with due diligence and planning to minimize risks and maximize your potential for success.

18. Local Businesses and Retailers

Partnering with local businesses and retailers can be a mutually beneficial way to source products for your ecommerce store. Many small businesses are willing to offer their products at wholesale prices to other businesses, allowing you to support your local economy while sourcing unique items for your online store.

19. Trade Shows and Exhibitions

Attending trade shows and exhibitions in your niche can be an excellent way to discover new products, meet suppliers, and stay up-to-date with industry trends. These events bring together manufacturers, wholesalers, and retailers, providing opportunities to network and establish business relationships. Attend relevant trade shows to find unique products and negotiate deals with suppliers.

20. Affiliate Programs and Dropshipping Marketplaces

Joining affiliate programs and dropshipping marketplaces can provide you with access to a wide range of products to sell on your ecommerce platform. Websites like AliExpress, SaleHoo, and Worldwide Brands connect you with suppliers and allow you to earn commissions on products sold through your unique affiliate links.

21. Subscription Boxes and Product Bundles

Creating your own subscription boxes or product bundles can be a unique way to source and sell products on your ecommerce store. Partner with manufacturers or wholesalers to curate a selection of complementary products that cater to a specific theme or niche. Customers love the convenience and surprise element of subscription boxes, and this model can help you secure recurring revenue.

22. Retail Arbitrage

Retail arbitrage is a popular **e-commerce strategy** that involves purchasing products from retail stores at a discounted price and reselling them online for a profit. This approach requires a keen eye for identifying profitable opportunities and a willingness to invest time and effort into sourcing and listing products.

To succeed in retail arbitrage, it's essential to be diligent in finding deals and discounts at local retailers. This may involve **regularly visiting stores**, monitoring clearance sales, seasonal promotions, and store closing events. Discount stores and dollar stores can be particularly fruitful sources for finding hidden gems that can be resold at a higher price.

When selecting products for retail arbitrage, consider factors such as demand, competition, and profitability. Look for items that are popular, have low competition from other sellers, and offer a good profit margin after accounting for all costs, including purchase price, shipping fees, and platform fees.

To determine the potential profitability of a product, compare prices on e-commerce platforms like Amazon and eBay. Use tools such as the Amazon Seller app or eBay's "Sold Items" feature to gather data on current selling prices and sales volume. This information will help you make informed decisions about which products to invest in.

Once you've sourced your products, create compelling listings that showcase the item's features, benefits, and condition. Use high-quality images and detailed descriptions to attract potential buyers and differentiate your listings from competitors.

If you are interested in this resale model, there is a great link to use to get a discount in the resources section of this book. It is the last chapter, right after chapter 8, titled Resources. I have a link to an extension that can save you a boatload of cash.

23. Wholesale Liquidation Auctions

Wholesale liquidation auctions are events where businesses sell off excess inventory, returned items, or slightly damaged goods in bulk. These auctions can be a great source for finding products at deeply discounted prices. Websites like Liquidation.com and DirectLiquidation.com offer access to online liquidation auctions, allowing you to bid on pallets or lots of products from the comfort of your home.

24. Surplus and Salvage Stores

Surplus and salvage stores specialize in selling products that are overstock, returned, or lightly damaged. These stores often offer products at significantly lower prices than traditional retail outlets, making them an attractive option for sourcing items to resell online. Be sure to carefully inspect the products for quality and condition before making a purchase.

25. Local Artisans and Crafters

Partnering with local artisans and crafters can be a great way to source unique, handmade products for your ecommerce store. Many artisans are looking for ways to expand their reach and are willing to work with online retailers to sell their creations. Attend local craft fairs, farmers markets, and art shows to connect with talented makers and discuss potential partnerships.

26. Eco-Friendly and Sustainable Suppliers

As consumers become increasingly conscious of environmental issues, sourcing eco-friendly and sustainable products can help set your ecommerce business apart. Look for suppliers that offer products made from recycled materials, organic or natural ingredients, or those that employ sustainable manufacturing practices. Partnering with these suppliers can attract environmentally-minded customers and contribute to a greener future.

27. Upcycled and Repurposed Items

Upcycling and repurposing involve transforming discarded or old items into new, functional products. This creative approach to sourcing can result in unique, one-of-a-kind items that appeal to customers looking for eco-friendly or quirky products. Consider learning a skill like woodworking, sewing, or painting to create your own upcycled items, or partner with artists who specialize in this craft.

28. Closeout and Liquidation Websites

Closeout and liquidation websites specialize in selling products from businesses that are closing, downsizing, or looking to clear out excess inventory. These websites often offer products at significantly discounted prices, making them an attractive option for sourcing items to resell. Popular closeout and liquidation websites include Closeout Central, Liquidation.com, and DollarDays.

29. Product Licensing and White Labeling

Product licensing and white labeling involve partnering with manufacturers to create products that bear your own branding or design. With product licensing, you can acquire the rights to use popular characters, logos, or designs on your products. White labeling allows you to sell generic products under your own brand name, giving you control over packaging and marketing. Both strategies can help you create unique products that stand out in the market.

30. Reverse Sourcing

Reverse sourcing is a strategy where you identify popular or trending products on ecommerce platforms and then work backward to find suppliers for those items. By using tools like Jungle Scout or Helium 10, you can research top-selling products on Amazon and other platforms. Once you've identified a product with high demand and profitability, reach out to manufacturers or wholesalers to secure a supply of that item for your own ecommerce store.

31. Consignment Inventory

Consignment inventory is a model where suppliers provide you with products to sell on your ecommerce platform, but you only pay for the items once they've sold. This arrangement can be beneficial for both parties, as it allows you to offer a wider range of products without upfront inventory costs, and suppliers can reach a larger audience without the risk of unsold inventory.

32. Local Farms and Producers

If you're interested in selling food products, partnering with local farms and producers can be a great way to source fresh, high-quality items. Many consumers are increasingly interested in supporting local businesses and eating locally-sourced foods. Reach out to farmers, beekeepers, cheesemakers, and other local producers to discuss potential partnerships and source unique, artisanal products for your ecommerce store.

Sourcing products for your ecommerce business is a crucial step in building a successful online venture. With the wide range of options available, from your own home to international suppliers, there's no shortage of opportunities to find unique and profitable items to sell. By exploring these 32 different sourcing strategies, you can diversify your product offerings, cater to specific niches, and build a thriving ecommerce business.

Remember to always prioritize product quality, customer satisfaction, and profitability when making sourcing decisions, and don't be afraid to get creative and think outside the box.

Happy sourcing, but keep reading… there is gold in them there hills.

Thank you so much for making it this far!

Thank you for taking the time to read my book. As a small indie publisher, your support means a lot to me. If you have just a minute after reading, I'd truly appreciate an honest review. I hope this book helps you make some fast money!

1. Open your smartphone's camera app.
2. Point your mobile device at the QR code.
3. Tap on the notification or screen prompt to open the link associated with the QR code.

Or

Visit https://bit.ly/MakeMoneyMel

Chapter 3: Selling on eBay

e**Bay is fun.** It is one of the most well-known and established online marketplaces. With millions of active users worldwide, eBay offers an incredible opportunity for sellers to reach a vast audience and build a thriving business. In this chapter, we'll dive into the essentials of getting started on eBay, explore the pros and cons of selling on this platform, and share best practices to help you achieve success.

Getting Started: To begin your eBay selling journey, the first step is to create an account. Visit eBay.com and click on the "Register" button in the top-right corner. You'll be prompted to provide your email address, create a unique username, and set a secure password. Once your account is set up, take some time to familiarize yourself with the platform's interface and navigation.

Next, it's time to start listing your items. eBay offers two main listing formats: auction-style and fixed-price (Buy It Now). Auction-style listings allow buyers to bid on your item, with the highest bidder winning at the end of the specified duration. Fixed-price listings, on the other hand, enable buyers to purchase your item immediately at a set price.

To create a listing, click on the "Sell" button at the top of any eBay page. You'll be guided through a step-by-step process where you'll provide information about your item, including the title, description, photos, pricing, shipping details, and payment methods. Take your time to fill out each section accurately and thoroughly, as this information will be crucial in attracting potential buyers.

When setting your price, consider factors such as the item's condition, market demand, and comparable listings on eBay. You can use eBay's "Completed Listings" feature to research recently sold items similar to yours, giving you a better idea of pricing trends and buyer expectations.

Pros and Cons: Selling on eBay comes with a host of benefits, but it's essential to weigh the pros and cons to determine if it's the right fit for your business.

Pros:

1. Large Audience Reach: With over 182 million active buyers globally, eBay provides access to an enormous potential customer base. This extensive reach can lead to higher visibility for your listings and increased sales opportunities.

2. Established Trust: eBay has built a reputation as a trusted and reliable online marketplace over the years. Buyers feel confident purchasing from eBay sellers, knowing that they are protected by the platform's buyer protection policies and secure payment systems.

3. Flexibility: eBay offers a wide range of product categories, allowing you to sell a diverse array of items. Whether you specialize in electronics, collectibles, fashion, or home goods, there's a place for you on eBay. The platform also provides flexibility in terms of listing formats, enabling you to

choose between auction-style and fixed-price listings based on your preferences and goals.

4. User-Friendly Tools: eBay provides a variety of user-friendly tools and resources to help sellers manage their listings and sales. From the Seller Hub dashboard, which offers insights and recommendations, to the eBay mobile app for on-the-go management, these tools streamline the selling process and make it easier to stay organized.

Cons:

1. Fees: One of the primary drawbacks of selling on eBay is the fees associated with using the platform. eBay charges various fees, including insertion fees (for listing items), final value fees (a percentage of the sale price), and optional feature fees (for upgrades like bold titles or subtitles). These fees can eat into your profits, so it's crucial to factor them into your pricing strategy.

2. Competition: Given eBay's vast user base, competition can be fierce. With numerous

sellers offering similar products, it can be challenging to stand out and attract buyers. You'll need to focus on creating compelling listings, offering competitive prices, and providing excellent customer service to differentiate yourself from other sellers.

3. Seller Policies and Restrictions: eBay has strict seller policies and guidelines that you must adhere to. Failing to comply with these policies can result in penalties, such as account restrictions or even suspension. Familiarize yourself with eBay's selling policies, including prohibited items, intellectual property rights, and seller performance standards, to ensure you stay compliant.

4. Time and Effort: Successfully selling on eBay requires a significant investment of time and effort. From creating listings and managing inventory to handling customer inquiries and shipping orders, there are numerous tasks to stay on top of. It's essential to be organized,

efficient, and dedicated to providing a positive buyer experience to succeed on the platform.

Best Practices: To maximize your success on eBay, implement the following best practices:

1. Optimize Your Listings: Create clear, concise, and compelling titles and descriptions that accurately represent your items. Use relevant keywords to improve search visibility and include essential details such as size, color, condition, and any unique features. Be honest about any flaws or imperfections to build trust with potential buyers.

2. Invest in High-Quality Photography: Visual appeal is crucial on eBay. Invest in high-quality, well-lit photos that showcase your items from multiple angles. Include close-up shots of important details, such as brand labels, tags, or any defects. Attractive and informative photos can make a significant difference in attracting buyers and encouraging sales.

3. Price Competitively: Conduct thorough research on eBay's completed listings to gauge the market value of your items. Price your items competitively to attract buyers while still ensuring a fair profit margin. Be open to negotiation and consider offering discounts for multiple purchases or repeat customers.

4. Offer Excellent Customer Service: Provide prompt, professional, and friendly customer service to build positive relationships with buyers. Respond to inquiries in a timely manner, address concerns with empathy and understanding, and go above and beyond to resolve any issues that may arise. Positive feedback and ratings from satisfied customers can greatly enhance your reputation on eBay.

5. Ship Promptly and Securely: Once an item is sold, prioritize prompt and secure shipping. Invest in quality packaging materials to protect your items during transit and consider offering multiple shipping options to cater to different buyer preferences. Provide tracking

information and keep buyers informed throughout the shipping process to maintain transparency and build trust.

6. Manage Your Inventory: Keep your inventory organized and up to date to avoid overselling or running out of stock. Utilize eBay's inventory management tools, such as the Seller Hub, to track your listings, monitor sales, and make data-driven decisions. Stay on top of your inventory levels to ensure a smooth and efficient selling experience for both you and your buyers.

7. Leverage eBay's Promotional Tools: Take advantage of eBay's promotional tools to increase visibility and drive sales. Utilize features like "Best Offer" to encourage buyers to make offers on your items, or consider running sales and promotions to attract more interest. Experiment with different strategies and track your results to optimize your approach over time.

8. Continuously Improve and Adapt: Stay informed about eBay's updates, policy changes, and seller resources. Continuously educate yourself on best practices, industry trends, and customer preferences. Be open to feedback and willing to adapt your strategies based on your experiences and insights. Continuously strive to improve your listings, customer service, and overall selling performance.

eBay's algorithm loves activity!!! Show it love, it will show you love! List baby!

Selling on eBay can be a rewarding and lucrative venture for those willing to put in the time and effort. By understanding the platform's basics, weighing the pros and cons, and implementing best practices, you can set yourself up for success. Remember, building a thriving eBay business takes patience, perseverance, and a commitment to providing value to your customers.

As you embark on your eBay selling journey, embrace the challenges and opportunities that come with it.

Don't be discouraged by setbacks or initial hurdles; instead, view them as learning experiences and opportunities for growth. Celebrate your successes, no matter how small, and use them as motivation to keep pushing forward.

One of the most valuable assets you have as an eBay seller is the community of fellow sellers and resources available to you. Engage with eBay seller forums, Facebook groups, and online communities to learn from others' experiences, seek advice, and stay updated on the latest trends and strategies. Attend eBay seller events and webinars to expand your knowledge and network with like-minded individuals.

Remember, success on eBay is not just about making sales; it's about building a brand and reputation that resonates with buyers. Focus on creating a positive and memorable experience for your customers, from the moment they encounter your listing to the time they receive their purchase. By prioritizing exceptional service and going above and beyond, you'll foster loyalty, encourage repeat business, and establish yourself as a trusted and respected seller within the eBay community.

As you grow and scale your eBay business, continue to adapt and evolve. Stay open to new opportunities, product niches, and strategies that align with your goals and values. Continuously assess your performance, seek feedback from buyers, and make data-driven decisions to optimize your listings and operations.

Chapter 4: Selling on Amazon

In the big world of e-commerce, Amazon reigns supreme, giving sellers a golden opportunity to reach a massive customer base globally. With tons of customers, efficient logistics, and a solid reputation, Amazon is the hotspot for entrepreneurs to grow an online business. Let's weigh the pros and cons of this powerhouse marketplace, and unpack key strategies for rocking it on the platform.

For assistance in setting up your account, there is a plethora of YouTube videos available at your disposal. I suggest you sort the results based on newest first just to ensure the information is most likely up to date.

Once your account is set up, it's time to start listing your products. Amazon offers several options for adding products to the platform:

1. <u>List a new product:</u> If you're selling a product that doesn't currently exist on Amazon, you can create a new product listing. This involves providing detailed information about the item,

including the title, description, images, price, and shipping details.

2. <u>Sell an existing product:</u> If the product you want to sell is already listed on Amazon, you can add your offer to the existing listing. This is known as "selling on a shared listing." You'll need to specify your price, shipping options, and inventory quantity.

3. <u>Use Amazon FBA:</u> Fulfillment by Amazon (FBA) is a service that allows you to store your products in Amazon's warehouses and have Amazon handle the shipping, customer service, and returns for your orders. With FBA, your products become eligible for Prime shipping, which can increase their visibility and appeal to customers.

Before you jump into one of these, check out the fee structure. There is definitely a higher cost to have Amazon fulfill your orders. Make sure what you're selling yields enough profit to justify this option. For more detailed information on the FBA option, YouTube University may be a great place to start. It's how I learned to sell on Amazon and utilize this fulfillment option. There are detailed videos on how to list, package, and ship your inventory to the warehouses.

When creating your product listings, it's crucial to provide accurate, detailed, and compelling information. Use clear, high-quality images that showcase your products from multiple angles and highlight any unique features or benefits. Craft detailed, informative descriptions that answer potential customer questions and emphasize the value your product offers.

Pros and Cons: Selling on Amazon comes with a range of advantages and challenges. Let's explore the pros and cons to help you determine if Amazon is the right fit for your business.

Pros:

1. Massive Customer Base: Amazon boasts over 300 million active customers worldwide, providing sellers with an unprecedented opportunity to reach a vast audience. This extensive reach can lead to higher visibility, increased sales, and rapid business growth.

2. Trusted Brand: Amazon has built a strong reputation for trust and reliability among consumers. Customers feel confident purchasing from Amazon, knowing that they are protected by the platform's customer service, refund policies, and A-to-z Guarantee. Selling on Amazon allows you to leverage this trust and credibility to attract and retain customers.

3. Streamlined Logistics: Amazon's fulfillment services, such as FBA, can greatly simplify your logistics and shipping processes. By leveraging Amazon's extensive network of warehouses and shipping partners, you can focus on sourcing and marketing your products while Amazon handles the storage, packing, and delivery.

4. Prime Eligibility: By using FBA or meeting certain seller criteria, your products can become eligible for Amazon Prime shipping. Prime customers are known for their high purchasing frequency and loyalty, and having

the Prime badge on your listings can significantly boost your sales potential.

5. Robust Tools and Analytics: Amazon provides sellers with a suite of powerful tools and analytics to manage their business effectively. From inventory management and order tracking to sales reporting and advertising options, these tools can help you optimize your listings, monitor your performance, and make data-driven decisions.

Cons:

1. High Competition: Due to Amazon's immense popularity among sellers, competition can be fierce. With numerous sellers offering similar products, it can be challenging to stand out and attract customers. You'll need to focus on optimizing your listings, pricing competitively, and providing excellent customer service to differentiate yourself from competitors.

2. Strict Policies and Compliance: Amazon has stringent policies and guidelines that sellers must adhere to. From product quality and

authenticity to shipping and customer service standards, Amazon closely monitors seller performance and compliance. Failing to meet these requirements can result in account suspensions, listing removals, or even permanent bans from the platform.

3. Limited Branding Opportunities: While Amazon provides a vast audience, it can be challenging to build a strong brand identity on the platform. Customers often associate their purchases with Amazon itself, rather than individual sellers. This can make it difficult to establish a loyal customer base and foster direct relationships with buyers.

4. Fees and Commissions: Selling on Amazon involves various fees and commissions that can eat into your profits. These include referral fees (a percentage of each sale), closing fees (for media items), and FBA fees (for storage and fulfillment). It's essential to factor these costs into your pricing strategy and ensure that you can maintain a healthy profit margin.

5. Dependence on Amazon: Building your business primarily on Amazon can create a sense of dependence on the platform. Changes in Amazon's policies, algorithms, or fee structures can significantly impact your sales and profitability. It's important to diversify your sales channels and consider expanding to other platforms or your own website to mitigate this risk.

Strategies for Success: To thrive as an Amazon seller, implement the following strategies:

1. Optimize Your Listings: Invest time and effort into creating compelling, informative, and keyword-rich product listings. Conduct thorough keyword research to identify the terms and phrases that potential customers are using to search for products like yours. Incorporate these keywords naturally into your titles, descriptions, and backend search terms to improve your visibility in Amazon's search results.

2. Prioritize Product Quality: Ensure that the products you sell on Amazon meet or exceed customer expectations in terms of quality, functionality, and durability. Source your products from reliable suppliers and conduct rigorous quality control checks before shipping them to customers or Amazon's warehouses. Consistently delivering high-quality products will help you build a positive reputation, generate favorable reviews, and foster long-term customer loyalty.

3. Competitive Pricing: Regularly monitor your competitors' prices and adjust your own pricing strategy accordingly. Use Amazon's pricing tools and automated repricing software to ensure that your prices remain competitive while still allowing for a reasonable profit margin. Consider offering promotions, discounts, or bundle deals to attract price-sensitive customers and encourage higher-value purchases.

4. Leverage FBA: If feasible for your business, consider using Fulfillment by Amazon (FBA)

to streamline your logistics and boost your sales potential. By storing your products in Amazon's warehouses and letting them handle shipping and customer service, you can save time and resources while providing customers with fast, reliable delivery. FBA can also make your products eligible for Prime shipping, which can significantly increase their appeal to Amazon's most loyal customers.

5. Encourage Product Reviews: Positive customer reviews are crucial for building credibility and trust on Amazon. Encourage your customers to leave honest reviews by providing exceptional products and service, and by following up with post-purchase emails or feedback requests. However, be sure to comply with Amazon's guidelines and avoid any attempts to manipulate or incentivize reviews, as this can lead to penalties or account suspensions.

6. Utilize Amazon Advertising: Take advantage of Amazon's advertising options to increase

your visibility and drive targeted traffic to your listings. Sponsored Products and Sponsored Brands allow you to place ads on search results pages and product detail pages, helping you reach customers who are actively searching for products like yours. Experiment with different ad formats, targeting options, and bidding strategies to maximize your return on investment.

7. Provide Exceptional Customer Service: Prioritize customer satisfaction by providing prompt, helpful, and professional customer service. Respond quickly to customer inquiries, address concerns with empathy and understanding, and go above and beyond to resolve any issues that may arise. By consistently delivering a positive customer experience, you can generate loyal repeat business, earn positive reviews, and build a strong reputation on the platform.

8. Monitor Your Metrics: Regularly review your key performance metrics, such as sales, conversion rates, customer feedback, and

inventory levels. Use Amazon's reporting tools and third-party analytics software to gain insights into your business performance and identify areas for improvement. Track your progress over time and make data-driven decisions to optimize your listings, pricing, and overall selling strategy.

9. Stay Up to Date: Keep abreast of Amazon's policies, guidelines, and best practices. Regularly review Amazon's seller central resources, attend webinars and events, and engage with the seller community to stay informed about the latest trends, strategies, and platform updates. Adapt your approach as needed to ensure compliance and maintain a competitive edge in the ever-evolving e-commerce landscape.

10. Expand Your Product Line: Continuously seek out new product opportunities and expand your offerings to diversify your revenue streams and attract a wider customer base. Conduct market research, analyze customer feedback and reviews, and stay attuned to

emerging trends and consumer preferences. By strategically growing your product line, you can reduce your dependence on any single product and build a more resilient and sustainable business on Amazon.

Remember, success on Amazon requires a combination of strategic planning, diligent execution, and ongoing optimization. It's not a get-rich-quick scheme, but rather a challenging and rewarding journey that demands dedication, perseverance, and a customer-centric mindset.

As you navigate the complexities of selling on Amazon, embrace the learning curve and view every challenge as an opportunity for growth and improvement. Seek out resources, connect with fellow sellers, and never stop learning and adapting to the dynamic world of e-commerce.

One key aspect of thriving on Amazon is building a strong brand identity, even within the confines of the platform. While Amazon may limit your ability to directly engage with customers, there are still ways to differentiate your business and foster brand loyalty.

Consider developing unique packaging, inserts, or branding elements that set your products apart and create a memorable unboxing experience for customers. Engage with customers through social media, email marketing, or your own website to build relationships and promote your brand beyond the Amazon platform.

Another critical factor in your success is staying organized and efficient in your operations. Develop systems and processes for inventory management, order processing, and customer service to ensure smooth and timely fulfillment. Leverage automation tools and software to streamline repetitive tasks and free up your time for higher-level strategy and decision-making.

As your business grows, consider expanding your reach beyond Amazon by exploring other e-commerce platforms, such as eBay, Walmart, or your own website. **Diversifying your sales channels can help mitigate the risks** associated with relying solely on Amazon and provide additional opportunities for growth and profitability.

Chapter 5: Selling on OfferUp

OfferUp is a **mobile-centric marketplace** that aims to simplify the process of buying and selling locally. Founded in 2011, the platform has grown to become one of the largest mobile marketplaces in the United States, with a strong presence in major cities and suburbs across the country.

At its core, OfferUp is designed to facilitate local transactions between buyers and sellers. Users can easily list items for sale by taking photos, writing descriptions, and setting prices directly from their smartphones. Buyers can browse listings, communicate with sellers through the app's built-in messaging system, and arrange to meet in person to complete the transaction.

Disclaimer: The author and publisher of this book do not assume any responsibility or liability for any risks associated with buyers coming to your house to purchase items from you. Hosting buyers at your residence carries inherent risks, including but not limited to personal injury, property damage, theft, or other unforeseen circumstances. It is the responsibility of the seller to take appropriate precautions to ensure their safety and the safety of their property. By choosing to invite buyers to your home for transactions, you acknowledge and accept these risks and agree to hold the author and publisher harmless from any claims or damages arising from such transactions. **Some alternatives** to having buyers come to your home are meeting them in public locations and even at police precincts. I have even met a buyer in front of my local fire station.

One of the key features of OfferUp is its emphasis on user profiles and ratings. Both buyers and sellers have public profiles that display their transaction history, ratings, and reviews from other users. This system helps build trust and transparency within the community, allowing users to make informed decisions about who they choose to interact with.

While OfferUp primarily focuses on local transactions, the platform has also **introduced a shipping option for certain items.** Sellers can choose to offer shipping on their listings, expanding their potential buyer base beyond their immediate area. However, it's important to note that shipping transactions may involve additional fees and logistics compared to local sales.

Pros and Cons: Selling on OfferUp comes with its own set of advantages and drawbacks. Let's explore both sides to help you determine if OfferUp is the right fit for your selling needs.

Pros:

1. Quick and Easy Listing Process: One of the biggest advantages of OfferUp is its streamlined listing process. With just a few taps on your smartphone, you can create a listing, upload photos, and start reaching potential buyers. The mobile-first interface makes it convenient to list items on the go, without the need for a desktop computer.

2. No Listing Fees: Unlike some other online marketplaces, OfferUp does not charge listing fees for most items. This means you can list your items for sale without incurring upfront costs, making it an attractive option for sellers looking to minimize expenses. However, it's

important to note that OfferUp does offer optional paid promotions to increase the visibility of your listings.

3. Local Focus: OfferUp's emphasis on local transactions can be a significant advantage for sellers. By connecting with nearby buyers, you can avoid the hassle and costs associated with shipping items, and you can often complete sales more quickly than on platforms that rely on long-distance transactions. Local sales also provide an opportunity to build connections within your community and establish a reputation as a trusted seller.

4. Large User Base: With millions of active users, OfferUp provides a substantial potential customer base for your listings. The platform's popularity means that your items can gain exposure to a wide range of local buyers, increasing your chances of making a sale. Additionally, OfferUp's user-friendly interface and mobile app make it easy for

buyers to browse and discover items they're interested in.

5. Flexibility and Control: Selling on OfferUp gives you a high degree of flexibility and control over your transactions. You can set your own prices, negotiate with buyers, and arrange meetups at times and locations that work best for you. This level of autonomy can be particularly appealing for sellers who value the ability to manage their sales on their own terms.

Cons:

1. No-Shows and Flaky Buyers: One of the challenges of selling on OfferUp is dealing with buyers who don't follow through on their commitments. No-shows, where a buyer fails to show up for a scheduled meetup, can be frustrating and waste your time. Similarly, some buyers may express interest but then ghost you or back out of the sale at the last minute. While this isn't unique to OfferUp, it's a common issue with local marketplaces.

TIP: When someone sends me a message asking if an item is still available, I say, "Yes, it is. I am located off of Broadway and the 15 freeway in the city of Flemming. What time are you available to come out?" If you don't do this, they will ask you for your address in advance, and then you are sitting around expecting them to show up. Once they give you a time and day, you can let them know, if it's not immediate, "Message me when you're about to leave, and I'll provide the address." I like to cut them off at the pass because I hate the feeling of sitting around expecting someone to show up.

2. Haggling and Low-Ball Offers: Because OfferUp is a platform for local transactions, it often attracts buyers who are looking for bargains. As a seller, you may encounter buyers who try to haggle aggressively or make low-ball offers well below your asking price. Dealing with these negotiations can be time-consuming and may require a firm stance on your pricing.

3. Limited Buyer Reach: While OfferUp has a large user base, its local focus means that your potential buyer pool is limited to your immediate area. If you're selling niche or specialized items, you may find it more challenging to find interested buyers compared to platforms with a wider geographic reach. However, this can be mitigated by using OfferUp's **shipping option** for certain items.

4. Safety Concerns: Meeting strangers in person to complete transactions always carries some level of risk. While OfferUp provides safety guidelines and encourages users to meet in well-lit, public locations, there is still a potential for unsafe situations. As a seller, it's crucial to prioritize your safety and take precautions when arranging meetups with buyers.

5. Limited Seller Tools and Analytics: Compared to some other e-commerce platforms, OfferUp offers relatively basic seller tools and analytics. While you can track your sales and

communicate with buyers through the app, you may not have access to advanced features like detailed sales reports, inventory management, or promotional tools. This can make it more challenging to scale your selling efforts or gain deep insights into your performance.

Effective Selling Techniques: To maximize your success on OfferUp, consider implementing the following selling techniques:

1. Craft Compelling Listings: Create listings that capture buyers' attention and provide all the necessary information they need to make a purchase decision. Use clear, well-lit photos that showcase your item from multiple angles and highlight any unique features or details. Write descriptive, honest titles and descriptions that accurately represent the condition and value of your item. Be transparent about any flaws or imperfections to build trust with potential buyers.

2. Price Competitively: Research similar items on OfferUp and other local marketplaces to determine a competitive price point for your listings. While it's important to price your items fairly, be prepared for some negotiation and haggling from buyers. Consider setting your initial price slightly higher than your minimum acceptable price to give yourself room to negotiate while still ensuring a fair profit.

3. Communicate Promptly and Professionally: Respond to buyer inquiries and messages in a timely and professional manner. Provide clear, concise answers to questions and be transparent about the condition and availability of your items. Use OfferUp's built-in messaging system to keep all communication within the platform, as this can help protect both parties in case of disputes.

4. Be Flexible with Meetups: When arranging meetups with buyers, try to be as flexible and accommodating as possible. Offer a range of

convenient times and locations that prioritize safety and accessibility for both parties. Consider meeting in well-lit, public places like coffee shops, shopping centers, or police station parking lots. If you're unable to meet at a buyer's preferred time, propose alternative options or suggest a different day that works better for you.

5. Practice Safe and Secure Transactions: Prioritize your safety and security throughout the selling process. Always meet buyers in person and avoid shipping items or accepting payment methods that can be easily reversed, like checks or money orders. If a deal seems too good to be true or a buyer makes unusual requests, trust your instincts and err on the side of caution. Consider bringing a friend or family member with you to meetups, especially for high-value items.

6. Build a Positive Reputation: Encourage satisfied buyers to leave positive ratings and reviews on your OfferUp profile. A strong reputation can help you attract more buyers

and command higher prices for your items. Provide excellent customer service, be honest and transparent in your dealings, and go above and beyond to ensure a smooth and satisfactory transaction for your buyers.

7. Promote Your Listings: Take advantage of OfferUp's promotional tools to increase the visibility of your listings. Consider using paid promotions like bumps or spotlight ads to showcase your items to a wider audience. Share your listings on social media platforms or local buy/sell groups to expand your reach beyond the OfferUp app.

8. Optimize for Search: Use relevant keywords and phrases in your listing titles and descriptions to improve your search visibility within the app. Think about the terms that buyers might use when searching for items like yours, and incorporate them naturally into your listings. Avoid keyword stuffing or misleading descriptions, as these can harm your credibility and violate OfferUp's guidelines.

9. Offer Bundle Deals: If you have multiple related items for sale, consider offering bundle deals to attract buyers and increase your average order value. For example, if you're selling a gaming console, bundle it with a few popular games or accessories to create a more compelling offer. Be sure to price your bundles competitively and highlight the value and convenience they provide to buyers.

10. Manage Your Inventory: Keep track of your active listings and sold items to avoid overselling or accidentally relisting sold items. Use OfferUp's mark-as-sold feature to remove items from your active listings once they've been purchased. Consider organizing your inventory and storage system to easily locate and retrieve items when it's time to meet with a buyer.

11. Handle Negotiations Tactfully: Negotiating prices is a common part of the OfferUp selling process. When buyers make offers or attempt to haggle, respond professionally and tactfully. If an offer is significantly lower than

your asking price, politely counter with a price that you're comfortable with, and be prepared to walk away if the buyer isn't willing to meet your minimum. Remember, it's okay to stand firm on your prices if you believe your items are fairly valued.

12. Embrace the Learning Curve: As with any new platform or selling experience, there will be a learning curve when getting started on OfferUp. Don't be discouraged if your first few listings don't sell quickly or if you encounter a few challenging buyers along the way. Use each experience as an opportunity to learn, refine your strategies, and improve your selling skills. Seek out resources, tips, and advice from experienced OfferUp sellers, and be open to adapting your approach based on your own trials and successes.

13. Diversify Your Offerings: While it's important to specialize in a particular niche or product category, consider diversifying your offerings on OfferUp to appeal to a wider range of buyers. If you have a variety of items to sell,

from clothing and electronics to home goods and tools, listing them all on the platform can help you reach different segments of the market and increase your overall sales potential.

14. Cross-Promote on Other Platforms: In addition to promoting your OfferUp listings on social media and local groups, consider cross-promoting on other online marketplaces and platforms. If you have a presence on platforms like Facebook Marketplace, Craigslist, or local buy/sell websites, share your OfferUp listings on those platforms as well. This can help you reach a broader audience and potentially drive more traffic and sales to your OfferUp profile.

15. Offer Exceptional Customer Service: Providing outstanding customer service is key to building a positive reputation and encouraging repeat buyers on OfferUp. Respond promptly to buyer questions and concerns, be transparent and honest in your communication, and go the extra mile to

ensure a smooth and satisfactory transaction. If a buyer has an issue with an item or transaction, work with them to find a fair and reasonable solution, such as offering a partial refund or replacement if warranted.

16. Stay Safe and Vigilant: While OfferUp provides a generally safe and secure platform for local transactions, it's essential to remain vigilant and take precautions to protect yourself and your belongings. Be cautious when sharing personal information, such as your phone number or home address, and always trust your instincts if a buyer or situation feels suspicious. If a buyer insists on meeting in a secluded or unfamiliar location, suggest an alternative public place or consider passing on the sale altogether.

17. Keep Accurate Records: Maintain accurate records of your OfferUp transactions, including buyer information, sale prices, and any relevant expenses like shipping or promotional costs. This can help you stay organized, track your profits, and ensure

compliance with any applicable tax or legal requirements. Consider using a spreadsheet or bookkeeping software to streamline your record-keeping process and make it easier to analyze your sales data over time.

18. Leverage OfferUp's Shipping Option Strategically: While OfferUp is primarily geared towards local transactions, the platform's shipping option can be a valuable tool for expanding your reach and selling to buyers outside your immediate area. When deciding whether to offer shipping on a particular item, consider factors like the item's size, weight, and fragility, as well as the potential shipping costs and logistics involved. Be transparent with buyers about shipping timeframes and any additional fees, and ensure that you package items securely to minimize the risk of damage during transit.

19. Build a Network of Local Sellers: Connect with other local sellers on OfferUp to build a network of like-minded entrepreneurs and potential collaborators. Attend local meet-ups

or join online forums and groups for OfferUp sellers in your area. These connections can provide valuable insights, support, and opportunities for cross-promotion or even bulk purchasing. Building relationships with other sellers can also help you stay informed about local market trends, pricing strategies, and best practices for success on the platform.

20. Continuously Improve and Adapt: The world of online selling is constantly evolving, and OfferUp is no exception. To stay competitive and successful on the platform, be willing to continuously learn, improve, and adapt your strategies based on your experiences and the changing market landscape. Stay up-to-date with OfferUp's latest features, guidelines, and best practices, and be open to experimenting with new approaches to listing, pricing, and promoting your items. Regularly seek feedback from buyers and fellow sellers, and use that insight to refine your selling techniques and optimize your performance on the platform.

Remember, success on OfferUp, like any other online marketplace, requires patience, persistence, and a willingness to learn and grow. Don't get discouraged by the occasional challenging buyer or slow sales period; instead, use those experiences as opportunities to build resilience, adaptability, and a stronger foundation for your selling business.

Chapter 6: Selling on Facebook Marketplace

Much like OfferUp, one of the key advantages of selling on Facebook Marketplace is its local focus. By default, your listings will be shown to potential buyers in your local area, making it easier to connect with nearby customers and arrange in-person transactions. This local emphasis can be particularly beneficial for selling large or bulky items that would be difficult or expensive to ship, such as furniture, appliances, or vehicles.

Disclaimer: The author and publisher of this book do not assume any responsibility or liability for any risks associated with buyers coming to your house to purchase items from you. See the tips in the previous chapter.

For a detailed walkthrough of setting up your marketplace account, you can always go to YouTube. That is where I learned how to do it. Just make sure you sort the videos based on date, with the newest first, so that you're provided with the most recent information.

When creating your listings, it's essential to provide clear and accurate information about your items. Use high-quality photos that showcase your items from multiple angles and in good lighting. Write detailed and honest descriptions that include relevant information such as the item's condition, dimensions, features, and any flaws or imperfections. Be transparent about your pricing and open to negotiation, as many buyers on Facebook Marketplace expect to haggle or make offers.

Once your listing is live, potential buyers can contact you through Facebook Messenger to ask questions, request additional information, or make offers. It's important to respond promptly and professionally to these inquiries, as timely communication can be key to building trust and securing a sale. Be clear about your availability for meetups or shipping arrangements, and always prioritize your safety when arranging in-person transactions.

Pros and Cons:

Like any selling platform, Facebook Marketplace has its advantages and drawbacks. Let's explore some of the key pros and cons to help you determine whether this platform is right for your selling needs.

Pros:

1. Large Local Audience: One of the most significant advantages of selling on Facebook Marketplace is the access it provides to a vast local audience. With over 2.7 billion monthly active users worldwide, Facebook is the world's largest social media platform, and a substantial portion of those users regularly browse and shop on Marketplace. This massive user base means that your listings have the potential to reach a wide range of local buyers, increasing your chances of making a sale.

2. No Listing Fees: Unlike some other online selling platforms, Facebook Marketplace does not charge any fees for listing your items. You can create as many listings as you want without incurring any upfront costs, making it an attractive option for sellers looking to minimize their expenses. This lack of listing fees can

be particularly beneficial for sellers who are just starting out or those who are selling lower-priced items that might not be profitable on platforms with higher fees.

3. Easy to Use: Facebook Marketplace is designed to be user-friendly and intuitive, making it easy for sellers to create listings and manage their sales. The platform's integration with Facebook means that you can use your existing Facebook account to access Marketplace, without the need for a separate login or profile. The listing process is straightforward, with prompts to guide you through adding photos, descriptions, and pricing information. Facebook's familiar interface and messaging system also make it easy to communicate with potential buyers and arrange transactions.

4. Social Connections: Selling on Facebook Marketplace allows you to leverage your existing social connections and network to promote your listings and build trust with potential buyers. When you create a listing on Marketplace, it can be shared on your Facebook profile, pages, or groups, exposing it to your friends, family, and followers. This social proof can help

to establish credibility and encourage buyers to purchase from you, as they may feel more comfortable transacting with someone who is connected to their own social circle.

5. Diverse Range of Categories: Facebook Marketplace supports a wide range of product categories, from furniture and home goods to electronics, clothing, and vehicles. This diversity means that you can list and sell almost any type of item on the platform, making it a versatile choice for sellers with varied inventory or those looking to declutter their homes. The platform's search and filtering options also make it easy for buyers to find specific items they're interested in, increasing the chances of your listings being discovered by the right audience.

Cons:

1. Safety Concerns: One of the main drawbacks of selling on Facebook Marketplace is the potential safety concerns associated with in-person transactions. Because most sales on Marketplace involve local meetups, there is an inherent risk in meeting strangers to exchange goods and money. While Facebook

provides some safety tips and allows users to report suspicious activity, it's ultimately up to sellers and buyers to take precautions and use their best judgment when arranging transactions. This can include meeting in well-lit, public locations, bringing a friend or family member along, and trusting your instincts if a situation feels unsafe.

2. No Seller Protections: Unlike some other online selling platforms, Facebook Marketplace does not offer any built-in seller protection or dispute resolution services. This means that if a buyer fails to pay, returns a damaged item, or makes a false claim, you may have limited recourse through Facebook itself. As a seller, it's important to document your transactions, communicate clearly with buyers, and be prepared to handle any issues that may arise on your own. In some cases, you may need to rely on external dispute resolution methods or legal action to resolve conflicts.

3. Limited Buyer Reach: While Facebook Marketplace has a large user base, its local focus means that your potential buyer pool is typically limited to your immediate area. This can be a disadvantage if you're selling niche or specialized items that may have a

smaller local market, or if you're looking to expand your sales beyond your region. However, some sellers may be able to mitigate this by offering shipping options or promoting their listings in Facebook groups or pages with a wider geographic reach.

4. Informal Setting: The informal and social nature of Facebook Marketplace can sometimes work against sellers, as buyers may be more casual or less committed to following through with transactions. Because Marketplace is integrated into a platform primarily used for social networking and communication, some buyers may approach transactions with a more relaxed or noncommittal attitude. This can lead to issues like no-shows, last-minute cancellations, or flaky communication, which can be frustrating and time-consuming for sellers.

5. Lack of Seller Tools: Compared to more specialized e-commerce platforms, Facebook Marketplace offers relatively basic tools for sellers to manage their listings and sales. While you can communicate with buyers through Facebook Messenger and mark items as sold, you may not have access to more advanced features like inventory management, sales tracking, or

promotional tools. This can make it more challenging to scale your selling efforts or gain detailed insights into your sales performance over time.

Optimizing Sales:

To maximize your success on Facebook Marketplace, consider implementing the following strategies:

1. Create Engaging Listings: Craft listings that capture buyers' attention and provide all the necessary information they need to make a purchase decision. Use clear, well-lit photos that showcase your items from multiple angles and highlight any unique features or selling points. Write descriptive and honest titles and descriptions that accurately represent the condition and value of your items, including any flaws or imperfections. Use relevant keywords and tags to help your listings appear in search results and be discovered by potential buyers.

2. Price Competitively: Research similar items on Facebook Marketplace and other local selling platforms to determine a competitive price point for your listings. While it's important to price your items fairly and account for their condition and market value,

be prepared for some negotiation and haggling from buyers. Consider setting your initial price slightly higher than your minimum acceptable offer to allow room for negotiation while still ensuring a fair profit.

3. Respond Promptly and Professionally: When potential buyers reach out with questions or offers, make an effort to respond in a timely and professional manner. Prompt communication shows that you're an attentive and reliable seller, which can help to build trust and encourage buyers to follow through with a purchase. Be clear and courteous in your responses, providing additional information or photos if requested. If a buyer makes an offer, consider it carefully and counteroffer if necessary, but always maintain a polite and respectful tone.

4. Be Flexible and Accommodating: Flexibility and accommodation can go a long way in creating a positive selling experience on Facebook Marketplace. When scheduling meetups or arranging transactions, try to be as flexible as possible with your availability and location preferences. Offer multiple options for meeting times and places, and be willing to work around a buyer's schedule if feasible. If a buyer

requests additional photos or information, do your best to provide them in a timely manner. Being accommodating shows that you value your buyers' time and needs, which can lead to more successful sales and positive reviews.

5. Leverage Facebook Groups: In addition to listing your items on Facebook Marketplace, consider promoting them in relevant Facebook groups or pages. Many communities have dedicated buy/sell/trade groups where members can post items for sale or search for specific products they're interested in. By sharing your listings in these groups, you can expand your potential buyer pool and tap into a more targeted audience. Just be sure to read and follow any group rules or guidelines regarding posting frequency, formatting, or member interactions.

6. Utilize Facebook Marketplace's Boosting Option: Facebook Marketplace offers a paid "Boost" feature that allows you to promote your listings to a wider audience beyond your local area. When you boost a listing, it will appear as a sponsored post in the Marketplace feed of users who match your target demographics or interests. This can be a useful tool for

increasing the visibility of your items and reaching potential buyers who may not have otherwise discovered your listing. However, keep in mind that boosting does come at a cost, so be strategic about which listings you choose to promote and set a budget that aligns with your selling goals.

7. Build Trust through Transparency: Transparency is key to building trust with potential buyers on Facebook Marketplace. Be upfront and honest about the condition of your items, including any flaws, damage, or wear and tear. Provide accurate measurements, dimensions, or specifications when relevant, and use clear, well-lit photos that show the item from multiple angles. If a buyer asks a question that you're unsure about, take the time to check and provide a thorough and honest response. By being transparent and forthcoming, you can demonstrate your integrity as a seller and create a more positive and trustworthy transaction experience.

8. Offer Bundle Deals or Discounts: If you have multiple related items listed on Facebook Marketplace, consider offering bundle deals or discounts to incentivize buyers and increase your sales. For

example, if you're selling several pieces of furniture, you could offer a discount for purchasing the entire set together. Or, if you have a collection of similar items like books or clothing, consider selling them as a lot at a slightly reduced price. Bundle deals not only provide value for buyers but can also help you clear out inventory more quickly and efficiently.

9. Promote Your Listings on Your Personal Profile: Facebook Marketplace allows you to easily share your listings on your personal Facebook profile, exposing them to your existing network of friends and followers. Take advantage of this feature by sharing your listings regularly, along with a brief description and any relevant details. Your personal connections may be interested in your items themselves, or they may know someone who is looking for something similar. By leveraging your social network, you can increase the visibility of your listings and potentially drive more sales.

10. Provide Exceptional Customer Service: Providing great customer service is essential for building a positive reputation and encouraging repeat buyers on Facebook Marketplace. Respond promptly to inquiries,

be patient and helpful in answering questions, and go above and beyond to ensure a smooth and satisfactory transaction. If a buyer expresses concern or dissatisfaction with an item, work with them to find a fair and mutually beneficial solution, such as offering a partial refund or discount on a future purchase. By prioritizing customer satisfaction, you can earn positive reviews and recommendations that can help to attract more buyers in the future.

11. Stay Safe and Secure: While Facebook Marketplace offers a convenient platform for local selling, it's crucial to prioritize your safety and security throughout the process. Always meet buyers in a well-lit, public location, such as a coffee shop or police station lobby, and consider bringing a friend or family member along for added protection. Avoid sharing personal information like your home address or financial details, and be cautious of buyers who make unusual requests or pressure you to meet in a private or isolated location. Trust your instincts and don't hesitate to cancel a meetup or transaction if something doesn't feel right.

12. Keep Accurate Records: Maintaining accurate records of your Facebook Marketplace transactions is important for both personal and tax purposes. Keep track of your sales, including the item sold, price, date of sale, and buyer information. This can help you stay organized, monitor your profits, and ensure compliance with any applicable tax laws or reporting requirements. Consider using a spreadsheet or bookkeeping software to streamline your record-keeping process and make it easier to analyze your sales data over time.

13. Follow Facebook's Commerce Policies: To maintain a positive selling experience on Facebook Marketplace, it's essential to familiarize yourself with and adhere to Facebook's Commerce Policies. These policies outline the types of items that are prohibited from being sold on the platform, such as illegal goods, counterfeit products, or items that violate intellectual property rights. They also provide guidelines for creating accurate and non-misleading listings, communicating with buyers, and completing transactions. By following these policies, you can help ensure a safe and trustworthy environment for both sellers and buyers.

14. Engage with Your Local Community: Facebook Marketplace provides a unique opportunity to connect with and contribute to your local community. Consider using your selling activities as a way to build relationships and engage with other community members. Attend local events or join community groups where you can network with potential buyers or other sellers in your area. Consider donating a portion of your sales to a local charity or cause, or offering discounts to community members in need. By being an active and engaged member of your community, you can build a positive reputation and create a loyal customer base for your Marketplace sales.

15. Continuously Improve Your Listings: To stay competitive and maximize your sales on Facebook Marketplace, it's important to continuously evaluate and improve your listings. Regularly review your active listings and assess their performance, taking note of factors like views, engagement, and sales. Experiment with different pricing strategies, photo styles, or description formats to see what resonates best with buyers. Seek feedback from successful transactions and use it to refine your listing approach and customer service. By constantly iterating and improving, you can

stay ahead of the curve and adapt to changing buyer preferences and market trends.

16. Expand Your Reach with Facebook Ads: While Facebook Marketplace itself is a powerful platform for local selling, you can further expand your reach and target specific audiences by using Facebook Ads. Facebook's advertising tools allow you to create sponsored posts that promote your Marketplace listings to users beyond your local area or personal network. You can target your ads based on demographics, interests, behaviors, and more, ensuring that your listings are seen by the most relevant and likely buyers. While running ads does require an additional investment, it can be a effective way to boost your visibility and drive more sales, especially for higher-value or specialty items.

17. Offer Contactless Payment and Delivery Options: In light of changing consumer preferences and public health concerns, consider offering contactless payment and delivery options for your Facebook Marketplace sales. Many buyers appreciate the convenience and safety of being able to pay electronically and receive items without face-to-face

interaction. Consider accepting payments through secure platforms like PayPal or Venmo, or using Facebook's built-in Checkout feature for transactions. For local deliveries, offer a "porch pickup" option where you leave the item at the buyer's door at a pre-arranged time. By providing these contactless options, you can make your listings more appealing to a wider range of buyers and demonstrate your commitment to their comfort and well-being.

18. Create a Consistent Branding Experience: Even though Facebook Marketplace is a more informal selling platform, creating a consistent branding experience can help you stand out and build a recognizable presence over time. Consider developing a simple logo or using a consistent color scheme and font in your listing photos and descriptions. Use a friendly and approachable tone in your communications with buyers, and consider including a short bio or tagline in your profile that reflects your selling style or values. By presenting a cohesive and professional image, you can create a more memorable and trustworthy impression that encourages buyers to seek out your listings in the future.

19. Collaborate with Other Local Sellers: Networking and collaborating with other local sellers on Facebook Marketplace can open up new opportunities and help you grow your sales. Join local seller groups or attend meetups to connect with others who are selling similar items or serving similar markets. Consider partnering with other sellers to offer bundle deals, cross-promote each other's listings, or even source inventory together. By building relationships and collaborating with other sellers, you can expand your knowledge, resources, and customer base, and create a more supportive and successful selling community.

20. Stay Informed and Adaptable: The world of online selling is constantly evolving, and Facebook Marketplace is no exception. To stay competitive and successful over time, it's important to stay informed about changes and trends in the platform and the broader e-commerce landscape. Follow Facebook's official Marketplace updates and announcements, and join online communities or forums where sellers share news, tips, and experiences. Be open to adapting your strategies and approach as needed based on shifting buyer behaviors, platform updates, or market conditions. By staying informed and adaptable, you

can position yourself for long-term success and growth on Facebook Marketplace.

Selling on Facebook Marketplace offers a unique and accessible opportunity.

Chapter 7: Selling on Etsy

At its core, Etsy is a marketplace dedicated to handmade and vintage items, as well as unique factory-manufactured items and craft supplies. The platform's mission is to connect buyers with independent sellers who offer products that are often difficult to find in traditional retail settings. Etsy's focus on creativity, authenticity, and supporting small businesses has helped it build a loyal and engaged user base of over 90 million active buyers worldwide.

Note: Although it deviates from Etsy's public persona, the platform has been allowing sellers to step outside of the handmade, vintage, and craft supply realm. They are allowing more and more mass-produced imported goods onto the platform. I love selling on Etsy and try to stick to their guidelines despite the reality on the platform. While you can get away with skirting its terms and conditions, I don't think it is worth the risk to my account.

If you seek a comprehensive guide on setting up an account, numerous detailed walkthroughs are available. Personally, I prefer visual aids as I am a visual learner; I find step-by-step demonstrations on platforms like YouTube very beneficial.

In addition to Etsy's listing fee (at the time if writing this book) of $0.20 per item, there is now a $15 charge for shop setup, as of the current time. For the most recent fee structure, please refer to the Etsy website.

When a buyer purchases one of your items, you'll receive a notification through your Etsy account and email. You'll then be responsible for processing the order, packaging the item, and shipping it to the buyer within your specified timeframe. Etsy offers various tools and features to help streamline your selling process, including integrated shipping labels, customizable order receipts, and detailed sales analytics.

Pros and Cons: Selling on Etsy presents a unique set of challenges and opportunities that differ from other e-commerce platforms. Let's explore some of the key aspects to consider when deciding whether Etsy is the right fit for your business.

Pros:

1. Fees: While Etsy's listing fees are relatively low compared to some other marketplaces, the platform also charges a transaction fee on each sale, as well as additional fees for certain services like currency conversion or advertising. These fees can add up over time and eat into your profit margins, especially if you're selling lower-priced items. It's essential to factor these costs into your pricing strategy and ensure that you're still making a sustainable profit after accounting for fees and expenses.

2. Competition: Etsy's popularity and growth have led to increased competition among sellers, particularly in certain product categories. With millions of active sellers on the platform, it can be challenging to stand out and attract buyers to your shop. You'll need to focus on creating unique, high-quality products, optimizing your listings for search, and providing exceptional customer service to

differentiate yourself from other sellers in your niche.

3. Maintaining Uniqueness: One of Etsy's core values is promoting unique, handmade, and vintage items. As a seller, it's important to ensure that your products align with this ethos and meet Etsy's handmade, vintage, and craft supply policies. This can be challenging if you're selling items that are similar to mass-produced goods or if you're considering scaling your production through outsourcing or manufacturing partnerships. It's crucial to maintain the integrity and authenticity of your brand while still finding ways to grow and sustain your business on the platform.

4. Intellectual Property Concerns: Due to the nature of handmade and creative goods, intellectual property issues can arise on Etsy. **Some sellers may inadvertently or intentionally infringe** upon copyrights, trademarks, or patents in their designs or products. As a seller, it's your responsibility to ensure that your items are original and do not

violate any intellectual property rights. Familiarize yourself with Etsy's policies on intellectual property and take steps to protect your own designs and ideas from infringement.

5. Balancing Creativity and Business: Many Etsy sellers are passionate creators and artists who may be new to the world of business and entrepreneurship. Running a successful Etsy shop requires a balance of creative skills and business savvy, including managing finances, handling customer service, and developing marketing strategies. It can be challenging to find the time and energy to focus on both the creative and administrative aspects of your business, especially as your sales volume grows.

Opportunities:

1. Niche Market: Etsy's focus on unique, handmade, and vintage items sets it apart from other e-commerce platforms and attracts a specific type of buyer. By selling on Etsy,

you have the opportunity to tap into a niche market of customers who value creativity, craftsmanship, and supporting independent artists. This can be particularly advantageous if your products cater to a specific aesthetic, style, or target audience that may be underserved by mainstream retailers.

2. Global Reach: With buyers and sellers from around the world, Etsy provides an opportunity to expand your customer base beyond your local area. The platform's international reach can help you connect with buyers who appreciate your unique products, regardless of their geographic location. Etsy's built-in tools for calculating shipping costs and handling currency conversions make it easier to manage global sales and reach a wider audience.

3. Community and Support: Etsy places a strong emphasis on community and supporting its sellers. The platform offers various resources, guides, and forums where sellers can connect, share advice, and learn from one

another. This sense of community can be invaluable for new sellers who are navigating the challenges of starting and growing their businesses. Etsy also provides educational resources, such as the Etsy Seller Handbook and online workshops, to help sellers improve their skills and succeed on the platform.

4. Customization and Branding: Etsy allows sellers to customize their shop pages and create a unique branding experience for their customers. By designing a cohesive and attractive shop banner, logo, and product listings, you can create a memorable and professional image that sets your business apart. Etsy's focus on individuality and creativity means that you have the freedom to express your brand's personality and story in a way that resonates with your target audience.

5. Potential for Growth: As your Etsy shop gains traction and builds a loyal customer base, there is potential for significant growth and expansion. Many successful Etsy sellers have

transformed their small-scale, home-based businesses into thriving, full-time enterprises. By continually refining your products, expanding your inventory, and investing in marketing and customer service, you can scale your Etsy shop and achieve long-term success on the platform.

Selling Tips: To maximize your success on Etsy, consider implementing the following strategies and best practices:

1. Develop a Strong Brand Identity: Creating a cohesive and recognizable brand identity is crucial for standing out on Etsy. Choose a shop name that reflects your products and personality, and design a logo and banner that visually represent your brand. Use consistent branding elements, such as colors, fonts, and imagery, across your shop page, product listings, and marketing materials. A strong brand identity helps build trust and loyalty with your customers and makes your shop more memorable.

2. Optimize Your Shop for Search: Etsy's search algorithm plays a significant role in determining which listings appear at the top of search results. To improve your shop's visibility, optimize your listings with relevant keywords, tags, and categories. Use descriptive and specific titles that include your primary keywords, and write detailed, informative product descriptions that highlight your items' unique features and benefits. Include high-quality, clear product photos that showcase your items from multiple angles and in use, if applicable.

3. Price Your Products Strategically: Pricing your products can be a delicate balance on Etsy. You want to ensure that you're covering your costs, including materials, labor, and Etsy fees, while still offering competitive prices that appeal to buyers. Research similar items in your category to get a sense of the market rate, and consider factors like the uniqueness, quality, and production time of your items when setting your prices. Don't undervalue your work, but also be mindful of

buyers' price sensitivities and willingness to pay for handmade or vintage goods.

4. Provide Exceptional Customer Service: Building a reputation for excellent customer service is essential for success on Etsy. Respond promptly and professionally to buyer inquiries, and be proactive in communicating about order status, shipping updates, and any potential delays. Pack your items with care and include a personalized thank-you note or small gift to surprise and delight your customers. Encourage satisfied buyers to leave positive reviews and feedback, which can help build trust and credibility with future potential customers.

5. Offer Customization and Personalization: Many Etsy buyers are drawn to the platform because of the opportunity to purchase unique, one-of-a-kind items that reflect their personal style and preferences. Consider offering customization or personalization options for your products, such as engraving, monogramming, or color choices. This can

help differentiate your items from mass-produced goods and create a more special and meaningful buying experience for your customers.

6. Leverage Etsy's Marketing Tools: Etsy provides various marketing tools and features to help sellers promote their shops and listings. Take advantage of Etsy's built-in social media sharing options to showcase your items on platforms like Facebook, Instagram, and Pinterest. Use Etsy's promoted listings feature to boost your visibility in search results for a small additional fee. Participate in Etsy's seasonal sales events and promotions, which can help drive traffic and sales to your shop during key shopping periods.

7. Engage with the Etsy Community: Etsy's community of sellers is one of its greatest strengths. Engage with other sellers in your niche by participating in Etsy Teams, forums, and local meet-ups. Share advice, collaborate on projects, and cross-promote each other's

shops to build relationships and expand your network. Attend Etsy-sponsored events, such as the Etsy Made in Canada market, to connect with buyers and showcase your products in person.

8. Offer Gift Options: Gift-giving is a popular reason for purchasing items on Etsy, particularly for occasions like birthdays, weddings, and holidays. Make it easy for buyers to purchase your items as gifts by offering gift wrapping, personalized notes, and direct shipping to recipients. Create curated gift guides or collections that showcase your items in a themed or occasion-specific way, and promote these during relevant gifting seasons or events.

9. Continuously Improve and Innovate: To stay competitive on Etsy, it's important to continuously improve and innovate your products, shop, and customer experience. Seek feedback from buyers and use it to refine your designs, materials, and production processes. Stay up-to-date with trends in your

niche and experiment with new techniques, styles, or product offerings to keep your shop fresh and relevant. Invest in your own skills and knowledge through workshops, courses, or mentorship programs, and apply what you learn to grow and improve your business.

10. Expand Your Reach Beyond Etsy: While Etsy can be a powerful platform for building your creative business, it's important to diversify your sales channels and not rely solely on one marketplace. Consider setting up your own website or online store to establish a more independent presence and capture customers outside of Etsy. Participate in local craft fairs, markets, or pop-up shops to connect with buyers in person and build brand awareness in your community. Explore wholesale or consignment opportunities with local boutiques or retailers that align with your brand and target audience.

Selling on Etsy can be a rewarding and fulfilling way to turn your creative passions into a thriving business. By understanding the platform's unique challenges and opportunities, and implementing strategies for success, you can build a loyal customer base, grow your sales, and achieve your entrepreneurial dreams. Remember that success on Etsy requires a combination of creativity, business skills, and perseverance, and that building a sustainable and profitable shop takes time and effort.

With each sale, each positive review, and each connection made on Etsy, you are not only building a successful business but also making a positive impact on the world by spreading creativity, beauty, and joy. Your unique voice and vision matter, and by sharing them on Etsy, you have the power to inspire and uplift others in ways you may never even know.

Chapter 8: Cross-Platform Selling Strategies

Managing Multiple Platforms: One of the key challenges of selling on multiple platforms is effectively managing your inventory, orders, and customer communications across different sites. Without a streamlined system in place, you risk overselling products, missing order deadlines, or providing inconsistent customer service, all of which can damage your reputation and bottom line. However, with the right tools and strategies, you can seamlessly handle sales across multiple platforms and reap the benefits of a diversified selling approach.

1. Inventory Management Software: Investing in a robust inventory management system is essential for cross-platform sellers. These tools allow you to sync your inventory levels across multiple sales channels, automatically updating stock quantities as orders come in and preventing overselling.

2. Centralized Order Management: In addition to inventory, it's crucial to have a centralized system for managing orders from multiple platforms. This can be achieved through multi-channel order management software, which consolidates orders from different sales channels into a single dashboard. These tools allow you to process orders, print shipping labels, and track fulfillment status across all your selling platforms, saving time and reducing the risk of errors.

3. Consistent Branding and Messaging: When selling on multiple platforms, it's important to maintain a consistent brand identity and messaging across all your sales channels. This includes using the same logo, color scheme, and product descriptions, as well as providing a similar level of customer service and communication. Consistency helps build trust and recognition with your customers, regardless of where they encounter your products.

4. Platform-Specific Optimization: While maintaining consistency, it's also important to optimize your listings and strategies for each individual platform. This means understanding the unique features, audience preferences, and search algorithms of each marketplace and tailoring your approach accordingly. For example, the product categories, listing formats, and buyer expectations on Amazon may differ from those on Etsy or eBay, requiring you to adapt your titles, descriptions, and pricing to suit each platform.

5. Streamlined Shipping and Fulfillment: Efficiently handling shipping and fulfillment is crucial for cross-platform sellers. To streamline the process, consider using shipping software that integrates with your sales channels and allows you to print labels, track packages, and manage returns from a single interface. Alternatively, you may choose to outsource fulfillment to a third-party logistics provider (3PL) that can store, pack, and ship your orders across multiple platforms.

6. Customer Service and Communication: Providing excellent customer service is essential for building a positive reputation and driving repeat business, regardless of the platform. When selling on multiple sites, it's important to have a system in place for managing customer inquiries, feedback, and returns across all your sales channels. This may involve using a centralized helpdesk or CRM tool, setting up platform-specific email templates, or designating a team member to handle customer service for each marketplace.

7. Data Analysis and Reporting: To make informed decisions and optimize your cross-platform selling strategy, it's crucial to track and analyze your sales data across all channels. Use the reporting and analytics tools provided by each platform, as well as third-party software that can consolidate data from multiple sources, to gain insights into your top-selling products, customer demographics, and overall performance. This information can help you identify trends,

adjust your pricing and inventory, and allocate resources to the most profitable platforms and products.

Legal and Administrative Considerations: In addition to the operational and strategic aspects of cross-platform selling, it's important to be aware of the legal and administrative considerations involved in running an e-commerce business across multiple channels. From tax obligations to business licenses and intellectual property concerns, sellers need to ensure they are complying with all relevant regulations and protecting their interests in the process. (**Don't let #1 scare you off.** Most platforms remit for you and in my state "economic nexus" is crazy high right now. If you need help, beyond your own online research, consult a tax professional.)

> Tax Implications: One of the most important legal considerations for cross-platform sellers is understanding and fulfilling their tax obligations. Online sellers are generally required to collect and remit sales tax for transactions in states where they have a significant presence or "nexus," which can be

triggered by factors like physical inventory, employees, or economic thresholds. When selling on multiple platforms, it's crucial to keep track of your sales and tax liabilities in each state and to register for permits and file returns as required.

In addition to sales tax, cross-platform sellers may also be subject to income tax on their e-commerce earnings. The specific tax implications will depend on your business structure, location, and the platforms you sell on. For example, marketplace facilitator laws in some states may require platforms like Amazon or eBay to collect and remit sales tax on behalf of third-party sellers, while other platforms may leave this responsibility to the individual seller.

To navigate the complex world of e-commerce taxes, it's recommended to consult with a qualified tax professional or use tax compliance software that can automate the calculation and filing process across multiple states and platforms. Failure to comply with tax regulations can result in penalties, interest, and legal consequences, so it's essential to prioritize this aspect of your business management.

Business Licensing and Permits: Another important legal consideration for cross-platform sellers is obtaining the necessary business licenses and permits to operate legally in your state and local jurisdiction. The specific requirements will vary depending on your location, business structure, and the types of products you sell, but may include:

- General business licenses

- Seller's permits or resale certificates

- Home occupation permits (if running the business from your residence)

- Professional licenses for certain regulated industries (e.g., food, cosmetics, or medical devices)

- Platform-specific seller accounts and agreements

To determine which licenses and permits you need, start by contacting your state and local business development agencies or consulting with a business attorney. Many states also offer online resources and guides for e-commerce businesses, which can help you navigate the licensing process and stay compliant with regulations.

Failing to obtain the proper licenses and permits can result in fines, penalties, and even the closure of your business, so it's crucial to prioritize this aspect of your legal obligations as a cross-platform seller.

> Intellectual Property Concerns: Intellectual property (IP) is another critical legal consideration for e-commerce sellers, particularly those who sell products across multiple platforms. IP refers to creations of the mind, such as inventions, designs, logos, and content, which are protected by legal rights like patents, trademarks, and copyrights. As a cross-platform seller, it's important to ensure that you are not infringing on the IP rights of others and that you are taking steps to protect your own IP assets.

Some key IP considerations for cross-platform sellers include:

- Avoiding counterfeit or knock-off products: Selling counterfeit goods is illegal and can result in serious legal and financial consequences, including account suspensions, fines, and lawsuits. Always source products from reputable suppliers and be cautious of deals that seem too good to be true.

- Respecting trademark and copyright laws: Be careful not to use trademarked logos, designs, or content without permission from the owner. This includes using brand names or logos in your product listings, as well as copying product descriptions or images from other sellers or sources.

- Protecting your own IP: If you have developed your own unique products, designs, or content, consider registering for trademarks, patents, or copyrights to protect your intellectual property from infringement by others. This can help you maintain your competitive advantage and prevent others from copying or profiting off your hard work.

- Monitoring for infringement: Regularly search for and monitor listings across different platforms to ensure that others are not infringing on your IP rights. If you discover instances of infringement, follow the platform's reporting procedures or consider sending a cease-and-desist letter to the infringing party.

- Seeking legal counsel: If you have complex IP concerns or are involved in a dispute, it's recommended to consult with an experienced IP attorney who can advise you on your rights and help you navigate the legal process.

By being proactive and informed about intellectual property issues, cross-platform sellers can avoid costly legal mistakes and protect their valuable business assets.

Platform-Specific Policies and Agreements: Each e-commerce platform has its own set of policies, terms of service, and seller agreements that govern the use of its marketplace and the behavior of its sellers. As a cross-platform seller, it's essential to carefully review and comply with these policies to avoid account suspensions, penalties, or legal issues.

Some common platform policies to be aware of include:

- Prohibited items: Most platforms have restrictions on the types of products that can be sold, such as counterfeit goods, hazardous materials, or illegal substances. Be sure to review each platform's prohibited items list and avoid listing any restricted products.

- Selling practices: Platforms may have specific guidelines around pricing, shipping, returns, and customer service that sellers are expected to follow. For example, Amazon has strict requirements around order fulfillment and customer response times, while Etsy prohibits the sale of mass-produced goods.

- Intellectual property: Many platforms have policies in place to protect intellectual property rights and prevent the sale of infringing goods. This may include procedures for reporting and removing infringing listings, as well as consequences for sellers who repeatedly violate IP policies.

- Fees and payments: Each platform has its own fee structure and payment processing system, which sellers must agree to when creating an account. Be sure to review the fees and payment terms for each platform you sell on and factor them into your pricing and budgeting decisions.

- Dispute resolution: Most platforms have processes in place for handling disputes between buyers and sellers, such as mediation or arbitration. Familiarize yourself with each platform's dispute resolution policies and be prepared to participate in the process if a dispute arises.

By staying informed and compliant with platform-specific policies, cross-platform sellers can maintain good standing on each marketplace and avoid legal or operational issues that could harm their business.

Data Privacy and Security: In today's digital age, data privacy and security are critical concerns for e-commerce businesses, particularly those that collect and process customer information across multiple platforms. As a cross-platform seller, it's important to understand your obligations under relevant data protection laws and to implement appropriate safeguards to protect your customers' personal information.

Some key data privacy and security considerations for cross-platform sellers include:

- Compliance with data protection laws: Depending on your location and the markets you serve, you may be subject to data protection laws such as the General Data Protection Regulation (GDPR) in the European Union or the California Consumer Privacy Act (CCPA) in the United States. These laws impose specific requirements around the collection, use, and protection of personal data, as well as the rights of individuals to access and control their information.

- Privacy policies and disclosures: Most e-commerce platforms require sellers to have a privacy policy that discloses their data collection and use practices. Your privacy policy should be clear, concise, and easily accessible to customers, and should cover topics such as what information you collect, how you use it, and how you protect it.

- Secure data handling and storage: Implement appropriate technical and organizational measures to protect customer data from unauthorized access, use, or disclosure. This may include using secure payment processors, encrypting sensitive information, and restricting access to data on a need-to-know basis.

- Third-party integrations and APIs: If you use third-party tools or integrations to manage your cross-platform sales, be sure to carefully vet these providers and ensure they have appropriate data protection measures in place. Regularly review and monitor your third-party integrations to ensure they are not introducing security vulnerabilities or compliance risks.

- Breach response and notification: In the event of a data breach or security incident, have a plan in place for containing the breach, investigating the cause, and notifying affected customers and authorities as required by law. Many data protection regulations impose strict notification requirements and timelines, so it's important to act quickly and transparently in the event of a breach.

By prioritizing data privacy and security in your cross-platform selling strategy, you can build trust with your customers, avoid legal and reputational risks, and create a more resilient and sustainable e-commerce business.

By investing in inventory management software, centralized order processing, and consistent branding and messaging, sellers can streamline their cross-platform operations and deliver a seamless experience for customers across all touchpoints. By carefully evaluating the pros and cons of each platform and matching their products and target audience to the right marketplaces, sellers can optimize their sales and profitability while minimizing competition and fees.

Resources

Note to my readers: When starting out with little to no money, it's advisable to minimize your investments. Some of the resources listed below cost money and may not be necessary for the level that you are at right now. Starting lean gives you the best chance at success.

Disclaimer: The information provided in this resource list is accurate as of the date of publication. Readers are advised that the specifics may have changed post-publication. The author is unaware of any fees associated with these resources. It is at the reader's discretion to determine if these resources fit into their budgets. The author assumes no liability for the use of any online or offline resources. Additionally, if I use the platform/service, I will link to a promo code when possible. Use the full link to be eligible.

Alright, **now that the legalese is out of the way**, let's get to the meat and potatoes.

The key with this section of the book is to check out some stuff that you might find helpful. Some are free, some are paid, some I have used, and others, my resale friends use. I have tried to categorize it the best that I can but there is some crossover so check out the entire list.

Cross Platform Selling Resources

1. **Crosslist** - Probably my favorite one of the bunch. A tool designed for quick and easy cross-posting between platforms like eBay, Poshmark, Mercari, and Depop. It focuses on simplifying the listing process with a streamlined interface. Use this link for any active promotion: https://bit.ly/crosslistmel

2. **Vendoo** - Vendoo is a tool that helps resellers manage their listings across multiple platforms like eBay, Poshmark, Etsy, and others from one place. It saves time and increases earnings by making it easy to import, delist, and relist items with a single click. Use this link for the promo: https://bit.ly/VendooMel

Pricing Resources

1. **Jungle Scout** - Tool for product research, demand, and competitive data. Visit: https://bit.ly/JungleScoutMel for the most current promotions.

2. **CamelCamelCamel** (Browser Extension) - A price tracker for Amazon listings. You can see price changes over time on a cool graph. Install from: camelcamelcamel.com

SEO Resources

1. **eRank** - Provides market trends, keyword suggestions, and listing audits. Visit: e-rank.com

2. **EverBee** - EverBee offers tools for Etsy sellers to find winning products, perform keyword research, and analyze competitors. Use link: https://bit.ly/EverbeeMel for the best possible promo.

Educational Resources

1. **Skillshare** - Offers a variety of online selling courses. Visit: https://bit.ly/SkillshareMel for a free month.

2. **The 4-Hour Workweek by Timothy Ferriss** This book will change your life! Insights into automating and optimizing online business operations.

Tools and Apps for Online Selling

1. **Honey** (Browser Extension) - This one is a **MUST** if you are using a **retail arbitrage model**. Automatically finds and applies coupon codes at checkout for online shopping. Install from: https://bit.ly/HoneyMelEids to get PayPal points which **convert into cash.**

2. **Pirate Ship** – Great shipping rates! pirateship.com

3. **Zoho Inventory** - Inventory management software that integrates with multiple online marketplaces. Visit: https://bit.ly/ZohoMel to check out the FREE plan.

Resources for Sourcing Products

1. **SaleHoo** - SaleHoo is the ideal product for customers who sell on eBay/Amazon, online stores and small businesses that are looking for trusted dropship and wholesale suppliers. The Directory contains 8,000 suppliers and 300,000+ products. This is my favorite place to source new products to sell. For the most current promotions available to my readers, use this link: https://bit.ly/SaleHooMel

2. **Alibaba** - For sourcing bulk items from overseas. Visit: alibaba.com

3. **AliExpress** - Offers a wide range of products at competitive prices. Visit: aliexpress.com

4. **Thomas Net** - Directory for finding suppliers and manufacturers in the US. Visit: thomasnet.com

5. **ImportGenius** - Provides data on international suppliers and competitors. Visit: importgenius.com

Thank you so much for making it this far!

I greatly appreciate the time you took to give my book a read. As a small indie publisher, it means a lot and I hope I'm making a difference in your resale journey.

If you have 60 seconds, hearing your honest feedback would mean the world. It does wonders for the book, and I love hearing about your experience!

4. Open your smartphone's camera app.
5. Point your mobile device at the QR code.
6. Tap on the notification or screen prompt to open the link associated with the QR code.

Or

Visit https://bit.ly/MakeMoneyMel

Made in United States
Troutdale, OR
12/02/2024